The Two Empires in Japan

A Record of the Church–State Conflict

by John M. L. Young

Crown & Covenant
PUBLICATIONS

© 1961 John M. L. Young
© 2011 Crown & Covenant Publications
7408 Penn Ave., Pittsburgh, PA 15208
info@crownandcovenant.com
www.crownandcovenant.com

The publishers gratefully acknowledge the generosity of Jane Young in this publication of her husband's work.

ISBN: 978-1-884527-36-4

Library of Congress Control Number: 2011943899

Printed in the United States of America
at McNaughton & Gunn, Inc., Michigan

Originally published by The Presbyterian and Reformed Publishing Company, Philadelphia, Pennsylvania, 1961.

All Scripture quotations, unless otherwise noted, are taken from the King James Version.

Cover design: Eileen Bechtold
Interior layout and copy editing: Linda Au Parker
Proofreading: Heidi Filbert

TO THE MEMORY OF
MY PARENTS,
who gave their lives for the proclamation of
the gospel of Christ their Savior in
Korea and Japan, 1905–1949.

Table of Contents

Acknowledgments

Through the years, ever since the days of our missionary experiences in the puppet empire of Manchukuo to the present, I have felt an inner and growing compulsion to write a record of the conflict between the Christian church and the polytheistic state in the Japanese empire. The record needs to be set straight, for there are those who have presented it with omissions and deviations which may be for the benefit of the compromising church but are not for the profit of the truth or posterity. Nonetheless, the work would probably never have been done were it not for the providential pressure of circumstances. On returning from furlough in November 1954, I was asked to address the autumn meeting of the Japan Bible Christian Council and chose this theme for my subject. The actual title was inspired by a book I had been reading on board ship, *The Two Empires* by B.F. Westcott. This title had been given the book after his death by his son, who took it from the appendix of his father's work on the Epistles of St. John, where he wrote of the church-state conflict in the Roman empire.

Following that lecture, the theme was expanded into a series of nine articles in *The Bible Times* [1955–1956] and would probably have stayed that way if it were not for some special circumstances. One was the many requests received for the articles to be published in book form. The other was that my son John, a senior in high school, had learned to type and was willing to work with me through the summer as I revised and expanded the material, typing the entire manuscript. To all of these I am extremely grateful.

In any work we do, it is frequently because of the efficient and unheralded labor of others behind the scenes that we are able to accomplish our task. This has certainly been the case with this book. The very first to be acknowledged with thanks for such work is my wife, Jean, without whose encouragement and efficient running of our family of nine during its writing it could not have been finished. It has entailed on her part many added duties as well as the loss of many hours of fellowship during the summer vacation. Another who is gratefully recognized is Miss Marian Bower, who graciously spent part of her summer vacation to proofread the manuscript and offer valuable suggestions. My heartfelt thanks is also due Samuel E. Boyle for consenting to write the foreword, and for his helpful suggestions, and those of Philip R. Foxwell, after reading the manuscript.

Still another who has helped tremendously is my colleague on *The Bible Times* staff, Miss Anne Wigglesworth, who has contributed much time to help proofread the printed text, as well as having read the manuscript. To my daughter Ruth also go my thanks for her work in helping prepare the bibliography. Acknowledgment must also be made to those who contributed the pictures, which I am sure will help the reader visualize the events described. Iwanami Shoten has furnished the pictures of the early Roman Catholic period. Mr. Koyo Kageyama of the Sun Photo has supplied the excellent pictures of the present remnant of the "Old Catholic" era, printed here for the first time, as well as the many excellent photographs of the prewar and war periods. Kyodo Photo Service supplied a number of the excellent postwar photographs. Special thanks are due Professor Takaya of Meiji Gakuin for loaning some of his pictures of the Hepburn era and for arranging the opportunity to photograph some of the library's rare manuscripts.

To busy missionary Clarence Young for lending his time and talents to design and do the cover for the [original] book goes my heartfelt appreciation. I feel he has caught and graphically portrayed in symbolic form the significance of the title.

It is the prayer of the author that God will use this book to help many better understand the actual situation in Japan and therefore better to work and pray for the winning of precious souls and the building of the Church of Christ in Japan.

—*John M. L. Young*
November 7, 1958

Foreword

Missions, whether foreign or domestic, is a difficult business. It inevitably produces conflict. Jesus said, "Do not think that I have come to bring peace to the earth. I have not come to bring peace, but a sword. For I have come to set a man against his father, and a daughter against her mother, and a daughter-in-law against her mother-in-law. And a person's enemies will be those of his own household. Whoever loves father or mother more than me is not worthy of me and whoever loves son or daughter more than me is not worthy of me. Whoever finds his life will lose it, and whoever loses his life for my sake will find it" (Matthew 10:34–39, ESV).

Jesus was speaking of the inevitable conflict that the gospel brings even in the family of one who abandons the futile ways inherited from their fathers and takes up his cross and follows Jesus. He was not speaking of the church taking up a sword in actual physical combat in violent conflict. As Paul by inspiration of the Holy Spirit makes clear, "For though we walk in the flesh, we are not waging war according to the flesh. For the weapons of our warfare are not of the flesh but have divine power to destroy strongholds. We destroy arguments and every lofty opinion raised against the knowledge of God and take every thought captive to obey Christ" (2 Corinthians 10:3–5, ESV). Missionaries preach and teach the gospel. Our weapons are words—reasonable arguments that are meant to persuade others to confess Jesus Christ as Lord. We rely on the Holy Spirit to press home the message of salvation and forgiveness of sins through Jesus Christ and faith in Him. Presenting the claims of Jesus Christ as Lord of all, however, confronts and causes offense to all forms of animism, idolatry, totalitarian nationalism, socialism and ancestor worship, as well as modern secular materialism. All are offended by a claim of loyalty and allegiance that is before and above all other loyalties and allegiances. And nothing less will do for the God who requires that we worship and serve Him only. There can be no compromise. Syncretism, compromising accommodations, or surrendering the uniqueness of Christianity for the sake of avoiding persecution or making the gospel more acceptable is out of the question. It is a subtle form of slowly being drawn into what will at last be a denial of our Savior and the transforming power of the gospel. It is not necessarily an easy thing to see the difference between a harmless cultural accommodation and a serious gospel-compromising one. Here is a perennial, ever-present problem in missions. And herein lies the timeless value of this book.

John M. L. Young's *The Two Empires in Japan* sets out timeless principles analyzing the real conflict that resulted when the kingdom of our Lord Jesus Christ was met with the defiance of the kingdom of this world personified in the emperor of Japan and Shinto shrine religion. Young sympathetically treats the mistakes and compromises, as well as the clear-eyed sterling testimonies with their terrible price to be paid for the sake of Christ. The book sets out the history behind the modern developments and the history that he himself lived through in Japan. Young gives us not theory alone but the doctrinal groundwork for standing firm for Christ in life's hard choices under persecution and the determined push back of a resistant culture. That is why I assign this book as required reading in my course on the enterprise of missions, titled the African and Asian Indigenous Church, at the Reformed Presbyterian Theological Seminary in Pittsburgh. Clear warning is signaled against well-meaning but sadly wrong choices so devastating to the true interests of the gospel and the well-being of the church and her testimony to Christ. The history of Christian missionary efforts is approached with understanding. The benefit of a thorough, historically rooted confessional foundation for newly formed indigenous churches is set out persuasively in an unembarrassed way.

The Japanese students that I have had the privilege to teach in the missions courses offered at the seminary have invariably responded favorably to this book, praising its accuracy, clarity, helpfulness and relevance. In a day such as ours in which there is rising again a form of renewed emphasis in Japan on Shinto religion and its public importance for the nation, the message and perspective of *The Two Empires in Japan* is timely and important. However, were that not the case, it stands the test of time as a case study that is applicable in the rest of Asia, Africa and the Middle East. And yes, there is also a painful relevance for the Western world as it increasingly shows itself hostile to all things Christian.

—*Pastor Steven F. Miller*
adjunct professor of missions, Reformed Presbyterian Theological Seminary
Pittsburgh, Pennsylvania
October 2011

Foreword

Mr. Hashimoto, governor of Osaka prefecture in Japan, recently in 2011 proposed to the Osaka prefecture legislation concerning the punishment against disobeying public school teachers. If they refuse to repent from their not participating of singing "*Kimigayo*" in the public school ceremony three times, proposed legislation flatly tells that they should be fired without condition. "*Kimigayo*" is the Japanese national anthem, which has been recently added in Japanese national legislation to promote Japanese patriotism. This tells of the emperor's eternal reign as the king, even using the illustration of "until the small stone becomes the huge rock." Mr. Okuno, an Osaka public school teacher, conscientiously has been refusing to sing this because of his faith in the true eternal King Jesus Christ, and had been punished already, but is facing the crisis to lose his position as an art teacher of a public school for the handicapped in Osaka. So as this book fully explains, the pressure of the national Shinto idea is vividly living in Japanese society even in the present time, and this is a sign of the need of many prayers for the spiritual fight that Japanese Christians face in Japanese society in various ways. Without knowing such deep spiritual battle, one cannot really recognize the reality of Japanese missions.

To build the church in Japan is a kind of work similar to building a fortress under severe unceasing attacks of the unseen and undermining enemy in a society. Do you think such a work is a waste of time and resources? Or do you understand such a fight is indispensable for the church of Jesus Christ at a certain stage of real development of His mission? Could you pray and support such a fight with patience and understanding until the world sees the real fortresses built in Japan in front of unceasing attacks of such spiritual enemy of Christ?

To really understand such problems in Japan missions, Pastor Young gives full and detailed explanations from history with many useful insights from the perspective of sound Reformed faith. To build a faithful Reformed church is the challenge of a practical and radical presentation of the saving gospel to the society, as well as of practical and radical responding to it in grace by obeying the Ten Commandments in praxis, regardless of any reactions from the society: refusing idol or ancestor worship, keeping the Sabbath day, teaching against marriage not in the Lord, avoiding worldly habits in relationship to the society, and faithfully observing the oaths or covenants taken before the Lord.

By God's grace, missionaries from the Reformed Presbyterian Church of North America had succeeded to build some fortresses here in Japan after World War II. But prayerful support is absolutely needed to avoid extinction or compromise.

This book starts by telling about God's knocking on the door of Japan three times: in 16th/17th century, then around 1867, and post-World War II. Then it tells about how the enemy's empire in Japan has responded to Christ's empire. Historical facts are so faithfully followed in detail, and very interesting, so this book could be a good textbook of Japanese church history, including the Roman Catholic Church. It describes well what kind of church the Japanese Protestant church had become.

You can sense and understand the pressure which exists behind the daily living of Japanese Christians from historical backgrounds. You may see the unseen enemy of Japan missions. Why had the Japanese church become powerless in the face of the pressure of the government before and during the World War II, and was still weak in spiritual battle even after the freedom of faith had been given widely?

The reason was its continuous bondage to the idol worship of emperor worship, Shintoism and Buddhism. It still continues in various ways. The theory of church growth cannot overcome the real spiritual disease here. The spiritual battle of obedience to the Lord of each Japanese Christian in family and living is at stake, which comes from the power of His living Word. This book draws the picture well about the difficulty of being awake in Japanese society in the spiritual midnight of idol worship. Everybody who desires to pray for Japan missions needs to understand this, if you desire to pray with clear understanding and patience. We Japanese Christians appreciate your prayers very much.

John M. L. Young is one of the founders of the Presbyterian Church in Japan (about fifty congregations mainly around Tokyo and the Nagoya area) as a member of the mission of the former Reformed Presbyterian Church Evangelical Synod. He has been especially a close friend of two missionaries of the Reformed Presbyterian Church of North America: Johannes G. Vos in Northeastern China and Samuel E. Boyle in Japan.

For further study, a short article by Johannes Vos, "Christian Mission and the Civil Magistrate in the Far East," has permanent value in analyzing the political and religious character of the government in Japan, which imposes such religious pressure on the society. (*Westminster Theological Journal*, Vol. III, 1940). It explains about the move of the Japanese government concerning national Shintoism in 21st century; there are three elements that the Japanese government has always used:

1) the control of education (public school text, etc.);

2) the participation in idolatrous rites (like singing "*Kimigayo*" or bowing towards Hinomaru, the Sun-flag);

3) the legislation of a law to control churches and missions.

And at the core of the problems of Japan missions there still lies the spiritual and societal atmosphere which has been nurtured by such a national Shintoism structure. This has continuously intimidated Japan missions for several centuries.

But we believe that the Lord can do anything even in Japan for His beloved church, and know that "yet in all these things we are more than conquerors through Him who loved us" (Romans 8:37, NKJV).

—*Shigeru Takiura, pastor*
Okamoto Keiyaku RPC, Japan Presbytery RPCNA
Representative, Kobe Theological Hall

Foreword

The *Two Empires in Japan* describes the conflict between Christianity and the ancient polytheistic culture of Japan as that struggle reached its climax in the relations between the Japanese church and the Shinto state. The book was written not as a history of Christianity in Japan but as a documented account of one important aspect of that history.

The author is well fitted to tell his story. Born in Korea of Canadian Presbyterian missionary parents, Rev. John M. L. Young grew up in the midst of the spiritual conflict which his book describes. During twenty-seven years spent in the Orient he has lived in Korea, Manchuria, North China and Japan, all but one year of this time being spent under the Rising Sun flag of Japan. The only time Mr. Young lived in an Asian nation not under Japanese rule was during 1948 when he served as a missionary in Nanking, China.

From Nanking, Mr. Young was transferred late in 1948 to Japan by his missionary board, the (American) Independent Board for Presbyterian Foreign Missions. In the past ten years in Japan he has served not only his own mission faithfully but also extended a strong influence for good among missionaries and Japanese pastors outside his own denomination as editor of the mission periodical, *The Bible Times*. Mr. Young is president of the Japan Christian Theological Seminary and has carried on evangelistic and pastoral duties with his colleagues in the Japan Christian Presbyterian Church. The interdenominational organization known as the Japan Bible Christian Council came into existence through the zeal of Mr. Young and other like-minded missionaries, and Mr. Young is currently its president.

The religious standpoint of the author is that of biblical theism as this faith is set forth in the *Westminster Confession of Faith*. He is a militant defender of historic Christianity and firmly holds to the faith that the Bible is the authoritative, inerrant, and verbally inspired Word of God, our only infallible rule for faith and practice. It is from this absolute biblical ground that the author views the struggles of the Japanese Christian movement under the state.

Mr. Young believes in a Christianity in full harmony with the Holy Scriptures and the creeds of the church. Because this faith is grounded in the very Words of Christ which will outlast the heavens and earth, because it rests on the Scriptures which Jesus said could not be broken, this must be the Christianity which triumphs in Japan. Any diluted substitutes cannot stand because the judgment of God is against them.

What is Christianity? Is the Bible true? Was Jesus born of a virgin? Did He work miracles as reported in the New Testament? Did Jesus shed His blood to atone for man's sins? Did the deceased body of Jesus rise from the dead as the New Testament teaches? These are crucial questions facing the church in Japan today. As men who claim to be Christians answer such questions affirmatively or negatively they shall be judged now and in eternity by God himself.

The attitude of the Christian churches toward paganism and idolatry stems from the churches' view of Bible truth. One main reason that most of the churches in Japan went down in defeat, during the temptation of state pressure to compromise with idolatrous worship in the recent war, was that the church's faith had already been undermined by Western modernistic scholarship. The "radioactive fallout" from the "atomic bomb" of European destructive criticism of the Bible has penetrated deeply into the very bones of the body of Christ in Japan today. This deadly poison has attacked the skull and backbone. Doubt and skepticism in the head produced deterioration in the courage to stand unto death for Christ. When the crisis came, the combined pressure of state persecution and inner weakness of faith brought almost the entire church to open sin in actual spiritual adultery with the worship of the mythical sun goddess of Japan. The burden to tell this tragic story, of much of which he was a witness, that the postwar churches might be warned and profited by the lessons of the past, rests heavily upon Mr. Young's conscience.

His purpose is not just to expose the past failures of others. Such defeats are narrated only because without these facts the true history of Christianity in Japan cannot be told nor the lessons of history learned. The author's real motive is to help all Christians working in Japan today to avoid such spiritual failure in the future. To furnish Christians with the material which will aid them to perceive the mistakes of the past, ought to be a sound contribution to enable them to avoid such pitfalls in the future.

Jesus Christ said to penitent Peter, who denied Him three times, "Simon, son of Jonas, lovest thou me?" When Peter's threefold confession showed his readiness for full restoration to service, our Lord said to him, "Feed my lambs."

When we read Mr. Young's record of the Shinto state's use of the public schools of Japan to force idol worship on all children, even children of Japanese Christians, our hearts will be distressed. Should we not think now of the future children of Japan? Our Lord says to the restored church in Japan now, "Feed my lambs." Is it not incumbent on Christian Japanese parents and pastors to do all in their power now to safeguard their religious liberty for themselves and their children? Is it not a solemn duty to train their children to stand, as Daniel stood against his temptation, if the future brings new trials to the Japanese churches? The central passion of the author of this book is to arouse the Christian forces in Japan now to rise up and defend their constitutional liberties, and to prepare now to be faithful by God's grace no matter what trials may yet come. "Exhort one another daily, while it is called Today: lest any of you should be hardened through the deceitfulness of sin. For we are made partakers of Christ, if we hold fast the beginning of our confidence to the end" (Hebrews 3:13-14).

It gives me great personal pleasure to recommend this book to the reader. Its wealth of quotations, bringing observations and facts from many sources, should prove of lasting value in furnishing source materials to those who wish to know the real situation of Christianity in Japan. It is my prayer that God will bless the message of this book to the Christians of Japan and to the Church in all the world.

—*Samuel E. Boyle, Reformed Presbyterian missionary and president*
Japan Bible Christian Council, 1956–'57
Kobe, Japan

Introduction

The river which stretched out below was a historical river. The antiquated wooden bridge which spanned it served as the western entrance of the ancient city of Hamheung, Korea. Early in the twentieth century, opening skirmishes of the first full-scale war between the forces of the West and the Far East had been fought along its banks. As some saw it, that was a war between an Empire of Christendom and the budding Empire of Shinto militarism. It was the corrupt empire of the former, Russia, however, which was soundly trounced. The victory of the latter set the way for the rapid expansion of the empire of Japan and settled the destiny of the little kingdom of Korea for the next two generations.

To those living in the mission compound overlooking the river, and to the Church they were striving to build in that northeast area of Korea, the coming of the Rising Sun flag, with the sun goddess ideology which accompanied it, had brought increasing problems. The hillside mission home had, on one occasion, witnessed a dozen black-uniformed policemen, workhorses of Imperial expansion, come into the servants' compound below to arrest a college youth who had dared in the 1919 Independence Uprising to shout for freedom and independence on the streets. The Mansei Revolt had been staged at the end of World War I, and had been participated in by many Christians, to impress the League of Nations with Korea's determination to be independent of the Japanese occupying forces and their empire. The young Christian college student's death from pneumonia, in the cold prison that winter, was but a symbol of the dying hopes of the independence movement as the League of Nations looked the other way.

Some thirty years later another battle was to be fought along that river for Korea's independence, this time between the alien power of Red China and the United Nation's U.S. Marines. The defeat and withdrawal from Hamheung of the overwhelmed Marines, and the subsequent truce signed by the United Nations at Panmunjom, again brought the expiration of the hope of freedom to north Korea, as well as personal tragedy and anguish to tens of thousands of Christians throughout the north.

One of the boys residing in the mission compound who watched the expansion of the empire of Japan in north Korea, later, as a young missionary, also watched its progress in Manchuria and north China. There he observed its head-on conflict with the Kingdom of Christ over the issue to whom a Christian owed his highest allegiance. He was to see some faithful Christians—his personal friends and neighbors—pass through a living death in prison, and at least one die, rather than bow their heads to do "distant worship" (*yohai*) to the emperor or the sun goddess's shrine.

One of his fellow missionaries, who suffered a court trial and cruel winter imprisonment for her faith, later wrote, "The octopus of State Shinto, the Japanese religion of Emperor and ancestor worship, had for years been reaching out with deadening grasp over all the empire, seeking to 'bind all their people into a unit,' but where it touched a child of the living, eternal God, it found resistance. It found a power it could not understand or master.... We and many of the Korean Christians made a solemn covenant with God that we and our households would have nothing to do with state Shinto worship. We realized this was resisting the law of the Government, but inasmuch as it touched the law of our God, we could do nothing else." [1]

That an expanding empire based on the concepts of "a divine emperor, a divine people and a divine land" should come into conflict with Christianity, is far from surprising. Nearly two millennia earlier, as the followers of Christ undertook the spread of the Christian gospel throughout the Roman Empire, that conflict broke out between the subjects of the Kingdom of Christ and the citizens of the pagan, emperor-worshiping state of Rome. The New Testament scholar B.F. Westcott has written a striking essay analyzing the causes of the inevitability of this conflict between the two empires of the church and the world, of Christ and of Rome. He gave the following four reasons for it: [2]

(1) Christianity is universal, crossing all national boundaries, while polytheism is national. (2) Christianity is absolute, exclusive in its claims for Christ over all, offering no compromise with other religions, while polytheism demands public participation in the state worship by all, regardless of whatever private convictions

or personal worship one might otherwise engage in. (3) Christianity is aggressive, holding that the old religions are, as Dr. Westcott points out, "positively false and pernicious. They must be assailed and not tolerated." (4) Christianity is spiritual and not temporal. "For the Christian the state was not the highest power. He owed allegiance to a greater Sovereign than the Emperor," wrote Dr. Westcott. In the empire of the world, the spiritual and temporal are completely confused, while the Christian must mark the sharp separation which our Lord presented when He declared, "Render unto Caesar the things that are Caesar's, and unto God the things that are God's" (Mark 12:17).

Collisions between Christian conviction and heathen practice were thus inevitable then, and still are today. The Christians within the Roman Empire would not worship the spirit, or genius, of a deceased emperor as was required by law, nor those living emperors who demanded worship. Instead they preferred to die, by the thousands, cruel deaths of torture. It was their positive conviction that the only way to preserve the life of the church of God was to die rather than compromise the purity of their confession. To the world, it looked as if this would lead to the complete destruction of Christianity and the church of God, but the amazing thing was that instead it led to Christianity's spreading like a mountain fire in a high wind. By A.D. 313 the emperors themselves were professing Christianity. In more recent times in this land, we have seen the effort to save Christianity and the church by compromising the purity of its confession, accommodating it to the demands of the state worship, with the result that instead of saving its life the church grew so weak that its life was almost extinguished. This of course, is nothing more than the principle enunciated by our Lord in Matthew 16:25: "For whosoever will save his life shall lose it: and whosoever will lose his life for my sake shall find it." History has indeed shown that in the time of persecution the church that tries to save its life by compromise with pagan demands will lose its life, while the church that is willing to lose its life in martyrdom, if necessary, will find its life preserved by a host of new believers. "The blood of the martyrs is the seed of the Church."

Missionaries who have returned after World War II are particularly interested in the course of "the two empires" in Japan. Twice great efforts were made to bring Christianity, in one form or another, to this island empire, and twice both efforts ended largely in failure. Now for the third time such an effort is being made, under the most favorable circumstances, with the greatest open door ever accorded Christianity in Japan. If success is to come now where others have failed, it must be gained through the efforts of the most discerning Christians who have ever labored for Christ under the Japanese flag. The record of the past efforts is both an example and a warning to all. To discern how to render to the non-Christian "empire of Caesar" the things that are due it, and yet never fail truly to render to God the things that are His and not Caesar's, requires men who are indeed "as wise as serpents and as harmless as doves." Such discernment is the need of the hour.

In the succeeding chapters, the attempt will be made to trace the development of the conflict between the two empires in Japan during the three periods mentioned above: 1549-1638; 1859-1945; and 1945 to the present. The lessons of history wait to be learned and effectively applied to the establishment of the cause of Christ today. May it not well be that the failures of the past lie principally in the inability properly to discern between the empires of Christ and the world; between the things that can be rendered to Caesar and the things that can be rendered to God alone?

----

1.   Bertha S. Byram, M.D., *God's Presence in a Japanese Prison*, p. 3. The Independent Board for Presbyterian Foreign Missions, Philadelphia, 1943.

2.   B.F. Westcott, *The Epistles of St. John*, Appendix I, p. 242 ff. Macmillan & Co., London, 1883.

納

Part 1:

The First Effort:

The Mission of the

Roman Catholic

Church

The Jesuit Trial and Failure

"The period of their success in spreading their religion by the sword was short lived, for soon the sword was taken up against them to their destruction."

The first men to come to the shores of Japan professing the Christian faith were shipwrecked Portuguese sailors in the year 1542 or 1543. Japanese historians record the arrival of the storm-driven vessel of Mendez Pinto and his men, off the southern island of Tanegashima, as being the first appearance of foreigners, Christianity, and firearms in their land. It was the latter in which they were particularly interested, and the sailors were urged to return with more of their powerful cannons. Before leaving, the Portuguese taught the islanders how to make arquebuses and in Japan this gun came to be known as Tanegashima. On one of their later trading visits, one of the Portuguese ships took a young Japanese named Anjiro back with it to India where he accepted the Christian religion as it was presented to him. In school one of his teachers, the priest Francis Xavier, a man with a restless, roving spirit, asked him if the Japanese people would readily turn to Christianity if they were to take it to them. His reply is

Francis Xavier and the cover of the version of The Imitation of Christ *used in Japan 1596.*

interesting: "They would investigate this religion by a multitude of questions, and, above all, by whether your conduct agreed with your words. This done, the *daimyos*, the nobility and the people would flock to Christ, being a nation which always follows reason as a guide." The two of them, together with another priest and two servants, set out for Japan, landing in Kagoshima, southern Kyushu, in August 1549.

They were well received and on calling on the southern *daimyo*, Xavier narrates that Anjiro "showed a beautiful picture he had brought from India, of the blessed Mary and the Child Jesus sitting in her lap. When the Prince looked upon it, he was overwhelmed with emotion, and, falling on his knees, he very devoutly worshipped it, and commanded all present to do the same."[1] These priests traveled far and wide, readily baptizing anyone who would consent, regardless of their knowledge, with the result that they could soon claim many converts. Xavier himself left within two years, dying a little later near Macao Island off the south coast of China. Other priests, however, came and within thirty years some 150,000 Japanese had been baptized and 200 churches established, the high water mark perhaps being double that in converts about the end of the century.

Internal Factors Aiding the Missionaries

Various factors contributed to the original phenomenal growth of the Roman faith during this period. One certainly must have been the utter forthrightness of Xavier's preaching. Japanese psychology has always tended to yield to one who speaks with authoritative certainty and the early missionaries made the most of this. Xavier hated idolatry and immorality, of which all kinds were on display everywhere in Japan. He did not hesitate to stand on the streets and denounce idolatry, sodomy, and abortion as the three greatest sins of the people of Japan. He denounced these sins before the very lords who practiced them, and frequently challenged the Buddhist priests to public debate, usually putting them to complete confusion with his Western logic and learning. Some of his converts of those first two years became zealous proclaimers of their new faith for the next forty years.

The missionaries' early success can also be partly attributed to the fact that a long period of civil warfare had left the common people poverty-stricken,[2] crushed in spirit and desperate for any change that signified hope. The native faiths proved themselves to the people to be destitute of help in the spiritual crisis that followed. Shintoism, the ancient cult of Japan, had little influence anymore while Buddhism, which had a firm grip on court life, had lost its influence with the masses, being morally bankrupt, and was openly opposed by the mighty warlord, Oda Nobunaga (1534-82). J.I. Bryan, writing of the civilization of that time, declared, "But religion, which had become itself military, trying to profit by the spoils of war, had little effect either morally or spiritually on that singing, dancing, poetizing society of sensual courtiers and their mistresses.... Even the monasteries quarrelled with each other and fought like feudal lords; and in one such monastic battle some 3000 monks were slain."[3]

To such religious chaos the Jesuits came offering all that the Buddhists gave at their best and more, as described so graphically by Otis Cary, "gorgeous altars, imposing processions, dazzling vestments, and all the scenic display of a sensuous worship—but they added to these a freshness and fervor that quickly captivated the imaginative and impressionable people. The Buddhist preacher—unless of the Shin sect—promised heavenly rest, such as it was, only after many transmigrations involving many lives. The Jesuit preacher promised immediate entrance into paradise after death to all who received baptism. There was little in the Buddhist paraphernalia that needed to be changed, much less abandoned. The images of Buddha, with slight application of the chisel, served for images of Christ. Each

Buddhist saint found his counterpart in Roman Christianity; and the roadside

Mariya Kannon (goddess of mercy), Mary and child sitting on a Buddhist lotus bud

shrines of Kannon, the Goddess of Mercy, were rededicated to Mary. Temples, altars, bells, holy-water vessels, censers, rosaries—all were ready and could be easily adapted to the needs of the new religion. To Japanese, accustomed to the thought of changing from one sect to another, this new change seemed slight."[4] There is little doubt but that during the preceding millennium Rome had copied extensively from the rituals of Buddhism. The reverse process was now found to

Japanese Christ of the Jesuit period

be without difficulty, as the images of Maria Kannon testified. All of this made it very easy for a Japanese to switch to the type of Christianity presented by the Jesuits, without giving up much of his Buddhist thought processes.

There was still another factor, however, greatly aiding the new missionaries. Oda Nobunaga, lord of Nagoya, in his wars to destroy the Ashikaga Shogunate and seize power over the whole land, sought the aid of the missionaries both for the arms they could import for him and for the help they gave him gladly but foolishly in his battles with the Buddhist priests. They encouraged his burning of the Buddhist temples and introduced the military principles of Loyola, which made it obligatory for *daimyo* converts to ban all pagan religions in their respective territories. By the end of Nobunaga's tenure some seventeen *daimyo* had adopted Christianity and made it compulsory in their areas. A Jesuit historian, Charlevoix, describes with approval how the spirit of the Inquisition was brought to Japan with the decree of these *daimyo* that all in their bounds must be baptized or leave in exile at once. "In 1577, the Lord of the island of Amakusa issued his proclamation by which his subjects—whether priests or gentlemen, merchants or tradesmen—were required either to turn Christians, or to leave the country the very next day.

"They almost all submitted and received baptism so that in a short time there were more than twenty churches in the kingdom." Again, "The first thing Prince Andrew (Lord of Arima) did after his baptism was to convert the chief (Buddhist) temple of his capital into a church, its revenues being assigned for the maintenance of the building and the support of the missionaries. He then took measures to have the same thing done in the other towns of his fief, and he seconded the preachers of the Gospel so well in everything else that he could flatter himself that he soon would not have one single idolator in his States."[5]

By such means the Jesuits sought to spread their faith in Japan. One historian was later to sum it up with these words, "The harvest was certainly great in proportion to the number of sowers. But it was a harvest mainly of artificial growth, forced by despotic insistence of feudal chiefs who possessed the power of life and death over their vassals, and were influenced by a desire to attract foreign trade."[6] They were soon to learn, however, that the militarism of the church was no match for the militarism of the paganism they faced. The period of their success in spreading their religion by the sword was short lived, for soon the sword was taken up against them to their destruction.

Hideyoshi the Great, 1536–1598

The first period of missionary activity in Japan coincided with the reigns of three of the most powerful rulers in the country's history, although the first two of these men never actually used the title *shogun* for themselves. Nobunaga was assassinated in 1582 (by one of his officers whose head he had tapped with a fan) and was succeeded by Hideyoshi Taiko Sama, "the great Counsellor," from 1583 to 1598, who had risen from being his stable boy to being his commanding general. He was a brilliant but utterly ruthless dictator who, although at first tolerating the missionaries, soon turned against them, and in 1587 proclaimed a decree of total expulsion for all the Jesuit priests, there being some 137 of them by that time.[7]

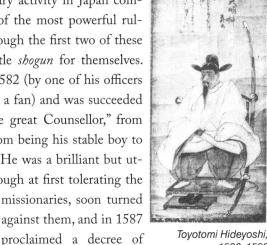

Toyotomi Hideyoshi, 1536–1598

Osaka Castle with original foundations laid in 1583 by Hideyoshi

Prior to the issuing of the edict of banishment, Hideyoshi sent five questions to Vice-Provincial Coelho, head of the Jesuit Mission. The second of these was: "Why have they [the Jesuits] induced their disciples and their secretaries to overthrow the temples?" And the third: "Why have they persecuted the *bonzes* [the Buddhist priests]?"[8] Coelho vigorously denied that they had engaged in any persecution of the Buddhists. The Japanese historian Kosaku Tamura, however, has written: "But there is a mass of evidence that the Fathers systematically instigated temple-wrecking and idol-breaking, and that the persecution of the *bonzes* was not confined to convicting them of error in the public debates."[9]

The fifth question was: "Why has he [Coehlo] allowed the merchants of his nation to buy Japanese to make slaves of them in the Indies?"[10] Charlevoix quotes Coehlo as replying, "The Fathers had left nothing undone to prevent the Portuguese from purchasing Japanese to sell them for slaves in the Indies." But Tamura cites

16th century Portuguese trading ship in Nagasaki harbor

a quotation from the archives of the Academy of History in Spain[11] which describes this heinous traffic in detail: "Even the very lascars and scullions of the Portuguese purchase and carry slaves away. Here it happens that many of them die on the voyage, because they are heaped up upon each other.... It even often happens that the Kaffirs cannot procure the necessary food for them. These scullions give a scandalous example by living in debauchery with the girls they have bought, and whom some of them introduce into their cabins on the passage to Macao. I here omit the excesses committed on the lands of the pagans, where the Portuguese spread themselves to recruit youths and girls, and where they live in such a fashion that the pagans themselves are stupefied at it."[12]

Coelho's answers were rejected by Hideyoshi and on July 25, 1587, his banishment of the foreign priests was posted in the following words:

> Having learned from our faithful councillors that foreign religieux have come into our estates, where they preach a law contrary to that of Japan, and that they have even had the audacity to destroy temples dedicated to our Kami [Shinto gods] and Hotoke [Buddha]; although this outrage merits the most extreme punishment, wishing nevertheless to show them mercy, we order them under pain of death to quit Japan within twenty days. During that space no harm or hurt will be done to them. But at the expiration of that term, we order that if any of them be found in our States, they shall be seized and punished as the greatest criminals. As for the Portuguese merchants, we permit them to enter our ports there to continue their accustomed trade, and to remain in our estates provided our affairs need this. But we forbid them to bring any foreign religieux into the country, under the penalty of the confiscation of their ships and goods.[13]

The effect of this edict was circumvented, however, by the priests withdrawing to Kyushu where, under the protection of the *daimyo* who had been converted to Roman Catholicism, they carried on a theological seminary as well as their preaching.

Five years later, a new development began to disrupt this status quo. Up to this time the Portuguese had had exclusive trading rights with Japan by virtue of a 1580 agreement with Spain and missionary rights by a Papal Bull of 1585. The missionary end was carried out by the "Society of Jesus," the Jesuits (co-founded by Xavier), who received their support from Portugal. Spain, on the other hand, monopolized the trade with the Philippines while the Franciscans, a Spanish order, were the missionaries there. In 1595, however, the Spanish Franciscans of Manila decided upon a stratagem for getting into Japan that circumvented both the Papal Bull and Hideyoshi's ban. The Spanish governor of the Philippines sent one of them, Pedro Baptista, to Hideyoshi as a commercial envoy and three others as his assistants. Within a year they succeeded in getting three more in and obtaining permission to build "The Shrine of the Angel Queen" for their use in Kyoto[14] where they were vigorously undertaking missionary work. They even went to Osaka to establish a convent, and two of them, on being sent to Nagasaki, began to conduct services in a Jesuit church there. When the Governor of Nagasaki forced them to return to Kyoto, they blamed the Jesuits for instigating this and criticized them to the Kyoto church members. Both the converted daimyo and new Jesuit bishop of Japan warned them to desist their missionary efforts but they continued. The resentment that was beginning to build up against them would have brought disaster even sooner had Hideyoshi not been fully preoccupied with his grandiose preparations to conquer China through Korea. The stubborn and resourceful resistance of the Korean navy, however, prevented the great warrior from getting beyond the north of that little Kingdom.

The Franciscan matter came to a sudden climax following the beaching of a great Spanish galleon, *San Felipe*, by the lord of Tosa who seized her rich cargo. The pilot in desperation tried to intimidate him by boasting of the might of Spain, pulling out a map to show him the great extent of the lands ruled by Philip II. When he was asked how his king had come by such vast possessions, the captain gave a very imprudent answer. "Our Kings begin by sending into the countries they wish to conquer religieux who induce the people to embrace our religion, and when they have made considerable progress, troops are sent who combine with the new Christians, and then our kings have not much trouble in accomplishing the rest."[15]

Lord Tosa saw that no time was lost in relaying these provocative words to Hideyoshi. His reaction was explosive. "What!" he cried. "My states are filled with traitors, and their numbers increase every day. I have proscribed the foreign doctors, but out of compassion for the age and infirmity of some among them, I have allowed their remaining in Japan. I shut my eyes to the presence of several others because I fancied them to be quiet and incapable of forming bad designs, and they are serpents I have been cherishing in my bosom."[16]

Portuguese portrayal of the crucifixion of 26 martyrs in Nagasaki, 1597

In his anger, Hideyoshi ordered that the three Franciscan friars in Osaka and three in Kyoto, with three Japanese Jesuits, plus seventeen of their converted servants, have their noses and ears cut off, be paraded through the streets of Kyoto, Osaka, Sakai, and Nagasaki, and be crucified in the latter city. The officer in charge, out of respect and pity for his victims, limited the work of mutilation to the lobe of an ear, but on February 5, 1597, the twenty-six martyrs died on crosses in Nagasaki. Hideyoshi also issued an edict prohibiting any *daimyo* from becoming Christians and reissued his 1587 ban on foreign priests. By that fall, however, only eleven Jesuits left, leaving 114 still in the country. The next year Hideyoshi's own life came to an end.

The Roman Cause under the Tokugawa Shogunate

After Hideyoshi's death in 1598, his chief general, Ieyasu Tokugawa, decided that he had the same right to displace Hideyoshi's son and heir that Hideyoshi had to slay Nobunaga's son and establish himself in his place. The Roman Catholic *daimyo* of the south backed Hideyoshi's son, but in the famous Battle of Sekigahara in 1600 they were soundly defeated and 40,000 of their men beheaded.

Ieyasu was at first not unfriendly to the foreign missionaries. His main purpose was to encourage trade with Spain, but when he found his friendship brought many priests but little trade, he became somewhat vexed. In 1611, his resentment was aroused by the discovery that a Spanish ship was exploring and charting his coasts. The Englishman Adams, retained in Edo, warned him that this could presage trouble from the aggressive Spaniards. That year, and again the next, he issued a proclamation declaring that "the religion of Kirishitan is proscribed under heaven." An incident probably contributing to this proscription occurred when a ship of Protestant Holland captured a Portuguese ship trading with Japan and seized a letter from Japanese Catholics to the King of Portugal asking for troops with which to seize control of Japan. During the next four years many Japanese converts were martyred, with more unknown numbers recanting their faith, and many churches were pulled down.

In 1616, Ieyasu died and his son, Hidetada, took over and intensified the persecution. Since 1597 no foreign priest had been executed in Japan, but now many were beheaded or burned at the stake. The climax came in 1622 when on one day, September 10, thirty converts were beheaded and twenty-five others, including nine foreign priests, were burned at the stake.

During the ensuing years of intense persecution many converted samurai, dismissed by their lords, wandered to areas in Kyushu that were almost completely Catholic. There too they found intense persecution underway, Ieyasu having replaced the Christian *daimyo* of Arima with a ruthless, anti-Christian tyrant. Denouncers of the "Beteren" [Padres] were given large rewards; those suspected of being believers were tortured to extract recantations or executed by a variety of excruciating methods. The sailing of Japanese ships abroad was prohibited and standing orders to execute any who attempted to leave or return were posted. Between 1614 and 1635, as many as 280,000 Christians are thought to have been persecuted for their beliefs. On top of all this, the *daimyo* of Arima imposed rigorous taxes in rice and seized and tortured those who did not pay. One of his methods was the "Mino-odori" [Mino dance] in which the farmer's straw raincoat was strapped onto his back, with his arms tied, and then set afire. Human flesh and spirit can only stand so much, and this terrible oppression of the masses finally brought an explosion.

The hounded, lordless samurai [ronin], together with the oppressed peasants, arose in revolt in December 1637, drove the lord of Arima and his nobles into his castle at Shimbara, and burned the town. When the inhabitants of the neighboring island of Amakusa, since 1577 almost entirely Catholic, heard the news, they immediately joined the uprising and drove out the *daimyo*'s officials. Although the revolt had both economic and religious origins, it at once received almost exclusive religious direction. A Catholic samurai young man of seventeen was chosen as leader and the decision was made for all joining in the resistance to withdraw to the abandoned castle of Hara, twenty miles south of Shimbara. Flags with crosses were flown from the walls and the cry went up that the time to avenge the blood of the martyrs had come.

By February 1638, the *shogun* had a massed army drawn up against them. The first two attacks of that month were repulsed with great loss for the attackers who then decided to wait until famine set in among the 37,000 defenders. On the night of April 11, a massive attack was launched by 100,000 troops, and the next morning the castle fell. Nearly all the Catholic leaders and samurai still surviving were there, with the result that, in the total massacre that followed, Catholicism was practically extirpated in Japan.

The ruins of the Hara castle symbolized the virtual extinction of the type of Christianity Rome had sent to Japan. Over two centuries later, when their priests

Edict board proscribing Christianity, offering rewards to informers, 1711

again returned to Japan, they could find only faint vestiges of it amongst some who still professed to believe as much of it as their fathers had preserved for them. Two years later, after the execution of the last Portuguese in Japan, the following inscription was posted: "So long as the sun shall warm the earth let no Christian be so bold as to come to Japan; and let all know that the King of Spain himself, or the Christian's God, or the Great God of all, if he violate this command shall pay for it with his head."[17] During the Tokugawa Shogunate, which continued for the next 250 years, a special police commission was organized called "the Christian Inquiry" and each year the Buddhist priests were required to report whether or not any Christians were known

Fumie

to live in their area. Before every large community, a sign board was erected proscribing the Christian religion. High rewards were offered for information leading to the seizure of believers, and those suspected were often called upon to tramp on a picture of Christ or Mary. In some areas special *fumie* were made of metal, with a picture of Mary, Christ, or a cross, to be tramped on as a sign of scorn for the Christian faith. Whole communities were sometimes called upon on New Year's Day to step on these *fumie*. It was with this bitter hatred and ruthless suppression that the first Roman Catholic era came to a close in Japan.

Fumie with the face of Christ worn off by treading

An Appraisal of the Roman Effort

How shall we assess the Roman Catholic effort and the reasons for its failure? Certainly no fair appraisal can ignore the fact that they were successful in making disciples, many of them. They seemed, however, to be more the disciples of a cause—the Christian religion—than the disciples of a Person, Jesus Christ. Once they had committed themselves to this cause, in true samurai fashion the more noble of them were willing to go all the way, even to death. To sacrifice one's all for "the cause," even his life, without restraint or complaint, was the essence of *bushido*, the way of the warrior. The Catholic missionaries were remarkably successful in getting many to transfer this devotion to the religion they brought from the West.

What then was the key to this success? Perhaps these three words could sum it up as well as any: knowledge, zeal and forthrightness. Their missionaries were educated men who had knowledge of the world's learning and of their own religion. They quickly applied themselves to learning the language of the people and their heathen religious beliefs. They had a burning zeal for their own faith based upon

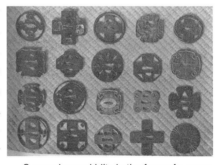

Samurai sword hilts in the form of a cross

deep convictions. This showed impressively as they went everywhere, to the high and low, seeking to make converts. Their sincerity and concern were apparent to all. With their knowledge and zeal they were very forthright, aggressively attacking the false religions of the people and eagerly seeking to engage the Buddhist priests in public debate. They frankly pointed out the hopeless confusion and illogic of Buddhist thought as well as the inevitable moral corruption that must come from a religion without a concept of a holy God. To the highest lords in the land, they exposed and denounced this terrible moral corruption, which was visible on every hand. The Japanese greatly admired them for these characteristics, which thereby furnished a key with which to enter many a heart.

Inro (medicine pill box) with Catholic symbols inside

With such great assets, why then did they fail? Certainly of paramount significance was the fact that their "Christianity" was an idolatrous, superstitious, ceremonial one that a pagan Buddhist could accept without much change of form and little of heart. In their preaching and life the two empires of Christ and the world were not clearly distinguished in either the spheres of worship or government. Their almost complete inability to discern between a man's duties in the two kingdoms of the temporal and spiritual realms is quite apparent in their disciples' burning of Buddhist temples and slaying of their priests with the tacit approval of the missionaries; in their enforcing baptism upon all the subjects of the converted *daimyo* and bringing Inquisition-type persecution upon those who refused; and in their plotting with Portugal to bring in foreign troops to overthrow and seize the government.[18] This evil record within Japan, coupled with the history of their countrymen's conquests in the Philippines, Mexico, South America and elsewhere, was their undoing and bore ample testimony to the extent of their ignoring the command of Christ to "render unto Caesar the things that are Caesar's, and to God the things that are God's." The result was a proscription of all foreign missionaries from Japan for the next two hundred and fifty years.

"Where, however, were the Protestants of that time?" it may well be asked. Why were not the churches of Holland and England sending out Christian missionaries with their trading ships to Japan? In the very year Ieyasu died, the great Synod of Dort was meeting in Holland, but no undertaking of the Church's responsibility to send the knowledge of Christ and His saving gospel into every land stemmed from that conference. Had the Protestant churches sent out missionaries then, it is likely that the Japanese government would have permitted them, for it was only the politically aggrandizing religion of Spain and Portugal they dreaded.

They yearned for trade with Western powers and were ready to grant freedom of religion to non-political religions. If such missionaries, with the same sense of evangelizing strategy the Jesuits possessed, had been sent, Japan today might have been a great Christian influence in the Far East. How different then would have been the ensuing history!

As it was, when, two and a half centuries after the proscription of Christianity caused by Rome, the first Protestant missionaries came to Japan, they found the name of their Lord intensely despised throughout the land. One of the first to come wrote home that, after being here a few years, her husband posted some Scripture verses in his dispensary. Then she added, "An intelligent Japanese said to him 'that these were excellent, all but the name of Jesus and that was very disgusting to a Japanese."[19] Ten years later the doctor wrote home, "I am fully persuaded that nothing but the fear of Romanism prevents the Japanese Government from according to the people full religious liberty. They feel that they can make no distinction between it and Protestantism, and they are afraid of it."[20] This then was the heritage of hate left to the new missionaries by the missionary effort of the Church of Rome.

If Christians today, however, are tempted to think, "Surely the fathers have eaten sour grapes and the children's teeth have been set on edge," let them also ask, "But what sacrifices are we making today to forward the gospel into every land?" The lessons of history are there for the learning.

---

1. Otis Cary, Japan and Its Regeneration, p. 52, Laymen's Missionary Movement, 1899.

2. The missionaries reported, in their Annual Letters to Rome, a "poverty so cruel that the destruction of children by their famishing parents was an every day occurrence." F. Brinkley, *A History of the Japanese People*, p. 534, the Encyclopedia Co., Ltd., N.Y., 1915.

3. J. Ingram Bryan, *The Civilization of Japan*, Williams & Norgate, 1927.

4. Cary, *op. cit.*, p. 53.

5. James Murdoch, *A History of Japan*, III vols., p. 92, 1903. Quotation from the Jesuit Charlevoix in his *Historie du Christianisme au Japon*.

6. Brinkley, *op. cit.*, p. 537.

7. Dr. Kosaku Tamura, "Japan's Foreign Relations," *Contemporary Japan*, Vol. XXIII, Nos. 1-3, 1954, p. 22.

8. *Ibid.*, p 19.

9. *Ibid.*, p. 17.

10. *Ibid.*

11. Quoted by Leon Pages in his *History of Christianity in Japan*, Annexe.

12. Tamura, *op. cit.*, p. 18.

13. E.W. Clement, *A Short History of Japan*, p. 69, University of Chicago Press, 1915.

14. T. Yanagita, *A Short History of Christianity in Japan*, p. 20, Seisho Tosho Kankokai, Japan, 1957.

15. Murdoch, *op. cit.*, p. 288.

16. *Ibid.*, p. 289.

17. Cary, *op. cit.*, p. 56.

18. R.H. Akagi, *Japan's Foreign Relations, 1542-1936*, p. 6, Hokuseido Press, Tokyo, 1936.

19. Mrs. Clara Hepburn writing to her Home Board in 1865. Quoted from M. Takaya, *The Letters of Dr. J.C. Hepburn*, p. 85. Toshin Shobo, Tokyo, Japan, 1955.

20. *Ibid.*, p. 135.

Part 2:
The Second Effort:
The Mission of the
Protestant
Denominations

2

The Protestant Churches Awaken to the Challenge of Japan's Need

"We want to train the native churches under our care to be governed by good, healthy laws and a sound creed, and to know the value of laws, and to submit to them."

By the middle of the nineteenth century, when Admiral Perry and his black ships had made successful contact with the Tokugawa Shogunate (1853), the situation in the great Protestant denominations had entirely changed. A new sense of vision and responsibility to fulfill Christ's great commission, to take His gospel to all the world, was beginning to stir them to missionary endeavor. The treaty of 1854 made between the United States and Japan had opened the door of trade slightly at two northern ports. This concession was followed in 1858 by another permitting foreigners to reside in several cities after mid-1859.

On May 2, 1859, the first Protestant missionary arrived and within a year seven were there from four different denominational mission societies: Protestant Episcopal, Presbyterian, Reformed, and

Admiral Perry's black ships as painted by a Japanese artist, 1853

Baptist, in that order. The door had been opened, however, by the shogun in Yedo (Tokyo) without the permission of the emperor in Kyoto, and the latter now began to demand that the foreigners be made to leave. The prime minister, Hotta, urged him to allow the foreigners to remain, giving a reason which became increasingly significant as the years passed. The Hotta Memorial to the Emperor in 1858 declared, "To have such a ruler (one to command universal vassalage) over the whole world is doubtless in conformity with the will of Heaven ... and in establishing relations with foreign countries the object should always be kept in view of laying a foundation for securing the hegemony of all nations.... Such a policy could be nothing else but the enforcement of the power and authority deputed (to the Yamato race) by the Spirit of Heaven."[1] In 1865 the emperor ratified the foreign treaties, but he lived after that only for another two years.

The new emperor was the young man under whose long reign ancient Japan was to be modernized, the Emperor Meiji (1867–1912). The progressively minded officials around him took the leadership and put great pressure on the young shogun, Tokugawa Keiki, to resign. This young man, caught between the pressure of the emperor's party on the one side and the foreigners on the other, decided to give up. The young progressives around the new emperor then decided, with the backing of the shogun's old southern enemies, the Satsuma, Choshu, and Tosa clans, to seize the palace on January 3, 1868. The reaction to this move was an instant one on the part of the Tokugawa supporters, and civil war broke out. The emperor's forces were victorious in the great battle of Fushimi, near Kyoto, and that November his court was moved to Yedo, the Shogun's seat of government, the name being changed to Tokyo.

Shintoism's Revival and the Meiji Restoration

The country's 270 *daimyo*, together with their 2,000,000 samurai, agreed to give up their rank and privilege, while the emperor promised to grant a national constitution with a parliament, govern through ministries, organize provinces under governors (many of whom were former *daimyo*), and form a new national army and navy. This change from feudalism to constitutional government was a bloodless revolution almost without parallel in its extent and suddenness. The Meiji Restoration, however, brought with it a great revival of Shintoism, which was treated as the state religion for the imperial government was considered to have its very foundation in the doctrine of the divinity of the emperor—a basic tenet of the Shinto faith.

During the first period considered, under the rule of the great shoguns, the chief religious opposition to Christianity came from the Buddhists. During this second period, under the reign of the emperors, however, the relentless religious opposition came from the Shintoists. What then was this newly revived religion of Shintoism? "The essence of Shinto is ancestor worship," states a pre-war government publication.

> Its 'Eight Million Gods' comprise the pantheon or great family of the Shinto deities. The greatest among these is Amaterasu Omikami, the Sun Goddess, and the Great Ancestress of the Imperial House. She is worshipped in the most venerated spot in Japan, the Great Shrine of Ise. Many members of the family of the Sun Goddess, as well as her descendants, are also worshipped by the Japanese people, who thereby show their boundless loyalty to the Imperial Throne. . . . It is from ancestor worship that the beautiful cult of filial piety was born. This virtue exists only in such countries as Japan that still have their old ancestor worship. Filial piety permeates the entire nation today. It means more than the devotion of children to their parents; it means the cult of the ancestors. According to it there must also be affection and respect among all members of the family, husband and wife, brother and sister, servant and master, as well as between the living and the dead. Nor is this all. Ancestor worship also means patriotism, loyalty to the Emperor and the State. A man who fulfills his duties to his ancestors will naturally be loyal to his friends and faithful to his prince.[2]

This worship of Amaterasu, the Sun Goddess, is a relic of the ancient sun worship familiar in so many lands, and the claim made for her as the original "ancestor" is but evidence of the lofty opinion the claimants had of their origin as being unique in the universe.

Shinto is the indigenous religion of Japan. The word itself means "the way of the gods." It has no official scriptures, no founder, no organized system of doctrine, and according to one of their scholars, "no morality to speak of; even the idea of purity is mostly ritualistic and physical."[3] The official U.S. Army General Headquarters report on the religions of Japan described Shinto this way: "As a religion it is concerned with a variety of deities, known as 'kami,' which vary in nature from the spirits of trees, foxes, and mountains, to deified ancestors, heroes, Emperors, and a pantheon of heavenly deities, chief among whom is the Sun Goddess. The worship of these 'kami' centers in the observance of ceremonies and festivals which are closely related to community and national traditions."[4]

This same report states that before the war there were some 110,000 Shinto shrines officially sponsored by the government, not counting thousands of small ones not so recognized nor the household shrines (*kamidana*, godshelves) in almost every home. Even today there are some 86,000 of these shrines affiliated in a postwar organization called the Shrine Association.

By far the most important of these shrines is that of the sun goddess at Ise, some three hundred miles southwest of Tokyo, located in magnificent grounds with giant cryptomeria trees native to Japan alone. This deity is held to have sent her grandson down to Japan to be the progenitor of the first emperor, Jimmu Tenno, the present emperor being held to be the 124th in direct succession. This event is said to have taken place in the 7th century B.C., although evidential Japanese history does not begin until about the 5th century A.D., some one thousand years later.

As a result of this belief, emperor worship has been one of the oldest traditions of the Japanese people. He was held to be a "living deity," incarnation of the sun goddess, and also chief Shinto priest of the nation. The Kashikodokoro, branch shrine of the Grand Shrine of Ise, stands near his former palace site where he still officiates regularly, as the newspapers periodically report. Throughout the medieval era the emperor was of little significance as a ruler, military dictators looking after that part of his duties. A literary study of the Confucian and Shinto classics (particularly the Kojiki and Nihonshoki, 8th century A.D.) in the late 18th century, however, laid the groundwork for the Shinto revival of the 19th century, which brought about the overthrow of the shogunate, the military dictatorship, and the restoration of the emperor to his place as ruler of the nation. The Meiji Restoration of 1868 was thus the product of a great Shinto revival and resulted in firmly establishing Shintoism as the national religion.

The Shinto zealots who brought about the Meiji Restoration were dedicated men and this soon became apparent in almost every branch of the reorganized government. The new constitution of 1889 proclaimed in its first article that the imperial family had ruled Japan for "ages eternal." The third article declared that the Emperor was sacred and inviolable. Thus the goal of these men was the establishment of a family-state based on worship of the sun goddess and the emperor as her living incarnation, "manifest deity." The word used to describe this unique form of government was *kokutai* [national structure], the cardinal principle of which was the worship of the emperor.

With the return of the Westerners and the Christian religion, the shogun's proclamations banning Christianity were replaced by those of the emperor and persecution increased for all who professed it or showed interest in it. It is estimated some 8,000 were persecuted between 1868 and 1873 with 2,000 dying in prison. The U.S. minister made many protests and finally, in 1870, was officially told by the foreign minister that "this government rested upon Shinto faith, which taught the divinity of the Mikado, that the propagation of the Christian faith and religion tended to dispel that belief, and that consequently it was the resolve of this government to resist its propagation as they would resist the advance of an invading army."[5]

Rev. James H. Ballagh and Mrs. Ballagh, early Reformed Church missionaries and founders of the first church

The pressure of international opinion, however, strongly voiced through the various embassies and governments abroad, had its effect and soon all the edicts banning Christianity were taken down, though the law itself was declared still to be in force. By 1880, as a result of a trend towards toleration, the missionaries found that they could, without molestation, rent halls for meetings and pass out literature. The first Protestant baptism in Japan took place in Yokohama on November 5, 1865, and the first church was organized there by Reformed Church missionar-

First Committee of Hepburn, Thompson and Ballagh started to work in 1867

ies Ballagh and Brown with eleven baptized members, in March 1872.[6] Its successor, the Kaigan Church, still stands by the present Yokohama South Pier.

During those early years of church organization,

Kaigan Church with tower added

Dr. & Mrs. J.C. Hepburn, first Presbyterian missionaries in Japan, 1859-1892

there were forces at work which were to have a far reaching influence on the history of the two empires in Japan. One of these was the strong nationalistic sentiment, quite apparent in the hearts of the early converts. The pioneer missionary of the Presbyterian Church, Dr. J.C. Hepburn, in writing home early in 1877 said,

They are thoroughly of the opinion that they can manage for themselves, and very jealous of foreign help, and foreign influence. This seems to be a national characteristic and is conspicuous in political and civil matters as well as religious.

First tract, translated by Hepburn, 1867. First gospel of Matthew, translated by Dr. Gutglaff

There is a great deal of national pride or conceit in them…. We see this feeling of taking the reins into their own hands very plainly in our churches. Most of the churches have suffered more or less from this disposition. I think the Congregational Churches about Kobe and Osaka are naturally doing the

Hepburn's John, revised by committee, cut in wood blocks, 1872. Hepburn's handwritten Romaji Matthew in back of dictionary manuscript.

same thing and their day of suffering is to come. It is all very well as long as they have their own way. The Presbyterian Churches, Scotch, Dutch and ours, are endeavoring to unite for mutual help and profit. I hope it will be successful. We want to train the na-

First edition, Hepburn's Matthew, 1873

tive churches under our care to be governed by good, healthy laws and a sound creed, and to know the value of laws, and to submit to them.[7]

Masahisa Uemura (1857–1925) and His Influence

By "sound creed" Dr. Hepburn meant the *Westminster Confession,* which was the creedal basis of the presbytery formed three years earlier by some of the missionaries, and their churches, of Presbyterian persuasion. The very first church founded, however, although started by a Reformed missionary, James Ballagh, had rejected such a comprehensive confession and based itself upon the brief statement of the World Evangelical Alliance, with an introductory statement which read in part: "Our Church does not belong to any denomination; its basis

Masahisa Uemura
1857-1925

is in the name of Christ alone, in whom all are one."[8] It called itself "the Japan Church of Christ Catholic" (*Nippon Kirisuto Kokai*). In its second year, young Masahisa Uemura, who was to become his church's most illustrious leader, joined it and under his influence the word "National" (*Koku*) was added to the name of the church, making it "the Japanese National Church of Christ Catholic" (*Nippon Koku Kirisuto Kokai*).[9]

First building (1874) of first congregation (1872), Yokohama, Kaigan

Most of the young men forming the early membership of this church came from militant samurai families and their strong nationalistic sentiment was much in evidence. The church begun in Tokyo in 1873 by Presbyterian missionary R. A. Thompson took the same name and creed as the Yokohama one at its origin. Another church begun in Tokyo that year, however, by Presbyterian missionary C. Carrothers, took the name Japan Presbyterian Church, and made its creedal basis the *Westminster Confession.*

Rev. David Thompson,
Presbyterian missionary,
arrived May 1863

In 1877, five churches that had carried this Presbyterian name and four carrying the Church of Christ title united to form the United Church of Christ in Japan (*Nippon Kirisuto Itchi Kyokai*). Ten years later their Synod had 85 delegates, pastors and elders, representing 57 churches present at its session.

In 1890, the Japanese leadership of this church, under the impetus of its most famous member, Masahisa Uemura, made a concerted effort to revise its Form of Government and Confession of Faith. These up to then had been the traditional Westminster Standards plus the *Canons of Dort* and the *Heidelberg Catechism*. Uemura became the champion for a brief and simple creed centering around the Apostles' Creed. His biographer states that he had a strong desire to see a national church founded, having "two cardinal points, the one being independence and the other non-denominationalism."[9] This meant that the church must be a Japanese one, independent from any foreign associations. His biographer put it this way: "As secular Japan was quite willing to sacrifice everything for national unification, so young Christians planned for an independent national church. Uemura ever stood for this principle and his convictions were never shaken."[10] It also meant that the Japanese church must develop a Japanized Christianity. Uemura himself gave the following description of that goal:

> The conservative theologians stick to the old creed and look back to the past. They hesitate to advance. I cannot agree with these people. Christianity is founded on historical facts. Further discussion of these facts is unnecessary, much less reform. But in such problems as the evidences of theism, theories of atonement, inspiration, how to interpret these facts, we must appeal to the Christian consciousness and the Bible. Under these lights, we find the virgin soil of theology before us waiting for our cultivation. Present day Christianity in Japan is in the period of propagation and needs no Confessions of Augsburg, Dort, or Westminster. Japanese Christians expect themselves to make advancement compatible with the culture of the nineteenth century. Therefore to introduce the old fossil-like creeds and sow the seeds of schism and division in the future is not a thing we can approve of. Christians in Japan therefore should make their Confession simple and liberal, leaving full room for development and at the same time furthering cooperation with other churches. The defects of a narrow creed will be more than we can tell.[11]

Uemura's conclusion as to what properly constituted the facts of Christianity was an inadequate one. If "Christ died" is a fact of Christianity, so also is it a fact that Christ died vicariously as a substitute to pay the price of the sins of all who would believe on Him, which is the doctrine of the substitutionary atonement. If the Bible's inspiration is a fact, so also is it a fact that its inspiration is verbal and plenary. To try to distinguish between these facts and declare some of them to be "facts" and some only theories is unsound. To choose the barest minimum of facts and to reject many of the others, declared to be the facts of essential interpretation by the great Reformed councils, some of the greatest assemblies of Christian scholars the world has ever known, as being unessential for the Japanese church might indeed open the way for the development of a Japanized theology but it could not be a biblical theology. The "non-denominationalism" and "independency" that Uemura sought for the Japanese church not only meant that it would have but a minimum of that creedal expression so essential to preserve a church from wandering off into erroneous paths of belief, but also that it turned its back on the fruitful doctrinal conclusions to which the Holy Spirit had led His Church through over eighteen hundred years of church history.

In one of his pleas for "the stronger denominations to unite into one powerful church," Uemura said, "The reason they [the earlier Japanese Christians] aimed to found a non-denominational church in Japan was that they found themselves a small army besieged by overwhelming hostile powers, eventually they thought it wiser to unite in essential faith, giving up trifles."[12] His biographer added, "For this reason they had nothing to do with Calvinistic theology or the *Westminster Confession*."

But it was just the Calvinistic conviction of the absolute sovereignty of God and absolute authority of the Bible as the Word of God, "the only infallible rule of faith and practice," which the Japanese church needed in its struggle with the demands of the polytheistic empire of the pagan state. The samurai's rendering of his supreme allegiance to his *daimyo* or the subject rendering it to his emperor, the Japanese mind understood full well, but the Calvinistic concept that a man's highest allegiance could be rendered to God alone, even though it meant disobeying his emperor, was lacking in the Japanese church as the struggle between the two empires intensified.

That Uemura himself had a sub-orthodox view of Biblical inspiration, one who was baptized by him has recently indicated with the following quotation from him: "The Bible was dynamically inspired, not verbally inspired.... We must never go to the extreme of worshipping the Bible as the very Word of God. The old saying 'Better to have no book at all rather than to swallow everything in it,' is apropos in this case also."[13]

The "powerful church" he sought through an increase of numbers by church union, which meant a mixed multitude of heterogeneous faith, would certainly mean the weakening of the church's doctrine. Weakening of doctrine, however, could only mean a weakening of the armor of defense against "the hostile powers" since it enabled liberals of many shades to enter. Such men lacked the strong convictions concerning truth and error necessary to enable the church to stand without compromise against the subtle blandishments of the polytheistic "hostile powers." History was to give a tragic demonstration of this.

The Impact of Hiromichi Kozaki (1856–1938)

Far to the south of the Tokyo-Yokohama area, in those early days of church organization, there was developing another unhappy illustration of the tragic consequence of blending the strong nationalistic sentiment of the young samurai with a belittling concept of the importance of detailed doctrine and biblical infallibility. In 1871, the *daimyo* of the Kumamoto clan in Kyushu had established a School of Western Learning to which a Christian American artillery captain of the Civil War, L.L. Janes, had been invited as principal. One of his early converts was Hiromichi Kozaki, a man destined to be recognized as the spokesman of Christianity in Japan, and, as such, recipient of the emperor's golden cups. He also became the first president of the National Christian Council, a position his son Michio Kozaki holds today. In his autobiography, Kozaki makes a number of interesting observations on the great influence the ideas of Janes had on the developing church through some of the young men he trained.

Capt. L.L. Janes, instrumental in the origin of the Kumamoto Band, 1876

This non-denominationalism has its root in our national character, for the first church established, that at Yokohama, for example, had in accordance with this same spirit called itself *Nippon Kirisuto Ko Kwai* (Japanese Christian Church

Catholic). Again, the young Christians of Kumamoto who formed a very great factor contributing to the rise of the *Kumiai* (Congregational) Churches were of the same spirit. The idea with which they had been most emphatically imbued by Captain Janes was that, unlike Europe and America, Japan had no need of denominations.[14]

Janes' view of the Bible also became that of his disciples. "Captain Janes had been sufficiently imbued with the scientific spirit to adopt the results of the higher criticism in his exposition of the Old Testament; he considered the Pentateuch not the work of Moses."[15] Again, "Though the higher criticism and the new theories as to the Bible proved a stumbling-block to many, I [Kozaki] remained unaffected because Janes had taught us that the Bible was not to be accepted as the literal truth at every point, and that, in particular, the Old Testament cannot be acepted as literal history."[16] To a conservative scholar Kozaki later stated, "I believe the main tenor of the teaching of the Bible but cannot accept the idea of its infallibility."[17]

In a single year's time, Janes succeeded in leading a number of young men to profess faith in Christ, who came to be known as the Kumamoto Band, including Ebina, Yokoi, Miyagawa, Kanamori, Harada, and Kozaki, all of whom became early leaders in the church. Yet every one of these men named defected to modernism and the first two, after returning

Mr. & Mrs. Tsuneteru Miyagawa, Mr. & Mrs. Danjo Ebina, and Mr. & Mrs. Hiromichi Kozaki

from American theological schools, became so permeated with modern unbelief that they demitted the ministry. Kanamori did also, although he later came to a real gospel experience with the Holiness and returned to preaching. As Kozaki himself declared, "The Bible, hitherto believed in as the infallible golden rule of conduct, had now begun to be treated by many as of little account."[18] Without the Bible to lean on as God's revelation of His will for men, they had to lean on their own novel ideas and those of others, and this they did. Christianity to them became more of a cause one joined than a Person to Whom one yielded his all and Whose written Word one believed and followed. As a result, accelerated apostasy could not but be expected.

The Japanized Christianity, resulting from the strong nationalistic sentiment and the rejection of the Bible as an infallible authority, took shape in different ways. Ebina taught that Jehovah was an ancient Shinto deity and he worked out a syncretism between Christianity and Bushido, "the way of the samurai," which was founded on the Confucian moral code. Another, Iwamoto, contrived a Buddhist Christianity while Matsumura founded a new religion called *Dokai* (The Way Society), which was a syncretizing of Christianity with Confucianism.

Modern descendants of the early Jesuit period carry on a syncretized worship outside of the Catholic Church.

With Kozaki, who was made president of the soundly conservative Christian educational institution Doshisha, on the death of its founder, Dr. Niishima, it eventuated in another way. His liberal influence and independent spirit, in that otherwise conservative school, resulted in an increasing trend towards liberalism and an increasing rupture with the evangelical missionary faculty. The crisis came in 1896 when Kozaki refused to make a declaration of his faith to satisfy a committee of inquiry sent out by the American Board, and all the missionaries resigned.[19] Kozaki later wrote, "I, in whom the missionaries had little confidence, and, what was perhaps of more importance, who differed from the most influential of them in theological views, often found myself in conflict with them even on the very important question of the religious education of the students."[20] From that year the usefulness of Doshisha to the cause of Christ rapidly declined until it became known as the center of radicalism in the areas of both theology and politics.

Following the organization of the first churches in Japan, the gospel spread rapidly until by 1884 some public leaders and statesmen were openly advocating that Christianity be adopted as the national religion, and that the emperor receive baptism. The skyrocketing popularity of Christianity, however, brought a great temptation to the young churches with the demand for membership by many who had other reasons than genuine faith for making the request. As a missionary of that period was later to write:

There were large additions to the churches and many were admitted whose mouths uttered devout confessions while their hearts were little affected by the truth. Looking back upon those days it is easy to see that with many persons the Christian religion was regarded chiefly as a means of advancing civilization and bringing good to the nation. Japanese preachers and foreign missionaries had much to say of the fruits of Christianity as shown in the history and present condition of Western lands. An appeal to patriotism was that which found the most ready response, and there was a temptation to use it too constantly. [*written in the late 1890s*][21]

The *Jiji Shimpo* ran a series of articles urging the nation to adopt Christianity on purely economic and political grounds, as the best thing for Japan ethically and socially. Observing the rise of this popularity one missionary wrote home to his board: "Japan is ripe for the Christian religion as no other nation is on the globe; and it is possible Japan may become Christian by royal decree in a day. The people, hungry for the gospel, crowd even the theaters to hear the preacher, and the whole aspect of missionary work in Japan is as fascinating as a romance."[22] That this was but a superficial and mistaken appraisal of the real situation, history was soon to demonstrate.

In that day there were some very serious failings. There was a noticeable failing to discern the strength of the grip of the religious cultural background upon the Japanese, with a corresponding inadequate testing of the professions made to see whether or not they were basically self-seeking or Christ-seeking. There was a common, erroneous appeal to accept Christianity for its superior fruits in a better civilization for Japan, rather than the preaching of the whole counsel of God. Further, the mistaken policy was also all too common of refraining from preaching the claims of Christ forthrightly over against those of the ancestral idolatry, the falsely optimistic view being held that the latter would fall off later since the people seemed to be so ready to accept Christianity. Finally, there was the failure adequately to take into account that the persistent demands for "independency" and "non-denominationalism" were all too frequently motivated primarily from a desire to adapt Christianity to the requirements of the Japanese nationalistic spirit. The fruit of these inadequacies was to be bitter in the years to follow.

---

1. Henry Satoh, *Lord Hotta, Pioneer Diplomat of Japan*, Tokyo, 1908.

2. Government Information, *Japan for the Young,* p. 54 f., Tourist Library series, 1934.

3. Genchi Kato, *A Study of Shinto, The Religion of the Japanese Nation*, p. 115, 1926. See also Ernest Satow, "The Revival of Pure Shinto," *The Transactions of the Asiatic Society of Japan,* Reprints, Vol. II, December 1927, Kyo Bun Kwan, Tokyo, p. 165. Address given 1882.

4. William K. Bunce, *Religions in Japan*, p. 99, GHQ, SCAP, C.I. and E. Section, Religious and Cultural Resources Division report, 1948 (published 1955). See P. Wheeler, *The Sacred Scriptures of the Japanese*, "Kami List (Deities and Personages)," pp. 363-84, 1952, H. Wolef, New York,

5. Cary, *op. cit.*, p. 81.

6. See M. Takaya, *op. cit.,* pp. 84, 181-2 and 120. Also K. Aoyoshi, *Dr. Masahisa Uemura, A Christian Leader,* Kyo Bun Kwan, Tokyo, 1940, pp. 24-7.

7. M. Takaya, *ibid,* p. 154-5.

8. Haruo Omura, "History of the Presbyterian Church in Japan," in *The Bible Times*, Vol. VII, No. 2, 1957, p. 4. Mr. Omura, an associate professor of philosophy in Tokyo's Metropolitan University, is intimately acquainted with this history, having been an elder in the Kaigan Church, as was his father before him.

9. K. Aoyoshi, *op. cit.*, p. 26.

10. *Ibid*, p. 65.

11. *Ibid*, pp. 77-8.

12. *Ibid*, pp. 26-7.

13. T. Tokiwa, in *The Presbyterian Guardian*. Philadelphia, December 1954.

14. H. Kozaki, *Reminiscences of Seventy Years*, p. 81, Kyo Bun Kwan, Tokyo, 1933.

15. *Ibid.*, p. 45.

16. *Ibid.*, p. 359.

17. *Ibid.*, p. 128.

18. *Ibid.*, p. 358.

19. See Sidney L. Gulick, *Evolution of the Japanese*, pp. 123-4, where he wrote, "The administration of the Doshisha became so distinctly non-Christian, to use no stronger term, that the mission felt it impossible to co-operate longer with the Doshisha trustees; the missionary members of the faculty accordingly resigned."

Fleming H. Revell Co., 1903.

20. H. Kozaki, *op. cit.*, p. 109.

21. Cary, *op. cit.*, pp. 91-2.

22. A. T. Pierson, *The Crisis of Missions*, p. 104, 1886, quoting J. T. Gracey, *Open Doors*.

3

Christian Education in Conflict with Shinto Ideology

The Rescript clearly put the emperor and his deity-ancestors in the place of God, and the Christian who professed to accept its doctrine had either to practice deception towards the nation or to his own God.

The decade that began in 1880 saw an amazing increase in the popularity of Christianity, but at its close a very noticeable reaction against the new faith set in. There were many in government posts who were there because of their devotion to the Shinto ideology, which had led them to bring about the restoration of the emperor to power. These "conservatives" were especially active in the Ministry of Education. They were much concerned over the great increase of Christian schools with the resultant turning of the nation's youth away from the ancestral gods, backbone of the "emperor system." To these vigorous proponents of the Shinto ideology, the nation's only real bond of union was the "emperor system," with its basis in absolute loyalty to the emperor and filial piety, which included ancestor worship. This meant that the whole nation must be bound together and governed by the concept of all yielding supreme and unquestioning loyalty to the emperor because of his divine origin and connection with the ancestral gods, who were held to have created the nation and provided for it from time immemorial. To these men, patriotism and devotion to the ancient pantheon of Shinto gods were inseparable, and the training of the youth of the nation in Christian principles, in opposition to the national polytheism, seemed to be the corruption of the empire at its very roots.

The Imperial Rescript on Education

In 1886, a new educational reform was announced which revealed that the government would increasingly take over in the field of education and that the religious-patriotic cult of Shinto would be disseminated through the educational system. Four years later, in 1890, the Ministry of Education announced what was to become perhaps the most damaging blow ever struck the Christian cause in Japan, the promulgation of the Imperial Rescript on Education and the initiation of special observances for reverencing the emperor. This consisted of making the "profoundest obeisance" before his portrait, and was an obligatory ceremony for all schools, Christian and governmental. The opening words of the Rescript were polytheistic to the core. They connected the origin of Japan to the activity of the mythological, ancestral gods and demanded "filial affection" to them as well as to their divine-human descendants. This "filial affection" to these divine "Ancestors" was declared to be "Our national polity" and "the true spring of Our Educational system." On special occasions the emperor's portrait was to be brought out before the whole student body of all schools, children and teachers were to be ordered to "make their profoundest obeisance before the portrait," the Rescript was to be read by the school president wearing white gloves, and then it was to be explained to the students.

Kanza Uchimura, 1861-1930

Although the government claimed that these observances were merely political and patriotic, it was obvious to many that they were far more than that. It was impossible to disassociate them from a significance which was religious in its very essence. One who recognized the obeisance as idolatry was the young man Kanzo Uchimura, who had returned from four years' study in Christian schools in America. He was teaching in the First High School of Tokyo and refused to do the obeisance to the Imperial Rescript and portrait beside it at the New Year's special services held in the assembly hall, January 9, 1891. Immediately he was charged with lese majesty and banned from all further teaching in schools. Who was this young man?

Kanzo Uchirnura (1861–1930)

Kanzo Uchimura, who was to become one of the most influential Christian thinkers and writers in Japan, was born of samurai parentage in Hokkaido in 1861. He entered the second class of the new agricultural school of Sapporo in 1877, and that fall, by the Christian students, was "forced to sign the covenant of the 'Believers in Jesus,'" prepared by Dr. William S. Clark, he states in his autobiography, *How I Became a Christian*.[1] The next year he was baptized by a Methodist missionary, Rev. M.C. Harris, and became a member of the Methodist Episcopal Church. Together with seven school chums he met for worship every Sunday in their private rooms. In 1880, their little "Sapporo Band" decided they would build a Methodist church but were dismayed to learn that the Episcopalians, who had come

Dr. William S. Clark

Covenant of "Believers in Jesus" of Sapporo Band

to town and had even baptized some of their classmates, were also contemplating building one. Uchimura wrote, "What is the use of having two separate Christian communities, when even one is not strong enough to stand upon its own feet? We felt for the first time in our Christian experience the evils of denominationalism."[2]

Although Mr. Harris, who had returned to the States, sent them money to build a Methodist church, Uchimura saw "no difficulty in separating ourselves from the existing denominations and in constituting ourselves into a new and independent body."[3] This was decided upon in 1881, and an agreement worked out with the Episcopalians, by which all their converts (plus the organ) would join with the Methodists in forming one, united, "independent native church," both parties leaving their respective denominations as soon as the Methodists were paid back. The church building was erected and dedicated early the next year, when the money was also returned. "Our independence was not intended as a revolt against Methodism," he wrote, "but as an expression of our real attachment to our heavenly Master, and of the highest sentiment of our love to our nation."[4] Here again the samurai's nationalistic sentiment can be seen to lie behind the desire for "independency" and for the building in Japan of a kind of Christianity which was somehow different from that of any existing denomination.

This can be seen even more clearly in the reasons he gave for not becoming an ordained minister. After graduating from Amherst College in New England in 1887, he was persuaded to attend a theological seminary. Of this he wrote:

> In a heathen country like mine, Christian ministers are supported either directly or indirectly by foreigners, and are to place themselves under the jurisdiction of foreign bishops of one kind or another.... No true countryman of mine suffers himself to be shackled by foreign influence of any kind ... and honor for myself and honor for my country had kept me from conceiving any idea whatever of entering into Christian ministerial service. Indeed, the first and greatest fear I had when I was first induced to accept Christianity was that they might make a priest out of me.... I made up my mind to study Theology, but upon one important condition; and that was that I should never be licensed.[5]

He left the seminary after three months and returned to Japan in 1888. Years later he was to write this further comment, "Now Rev. stands for Reverend, which means in common speech a licensed minister. But as I was never licensed to preach or to administer church ordinances by any church authority, I ought not to be called Reverend.... I was born a Japanese samurai; and the samurai detested *bozu* (priest) more than anything else ... I am not a *bozu*; my ancestors would be angry at me if ever I assume that title. So, my foreign friends will kindly refrain from addressing me as 'Rev.'"[6]

Uchimura became an ardent advocate of "Japanese Christianity" (*Nihon Teki Kirisuto Kyo*), of which he wrote, "It is Christianity received by Japanese directly from God without any foreign intermediary; no more, no less.... The Spirit of Japan inspired by the Almighty is Japanese Christianity. It is free, independent, original and productive, as true Christianity always is.... Only Japanese Christianity will save Japan and Japanese."[7] His particular form of it came to be known as *Mukyokaishugi* or "We-Need-No-Church Principle."

Its modern appellation is *Mukyokai*, or Non-Church Movement, and it is frequently estimated as now having a following as high as 50,000 to 70,000.[8]

However, one of its modern leaders, Toshiro Suzuki, estimates its present numerical strength as being closer to 5,000.[9] It is a highly intellectual movement today, stressing biblical exegesis and permeated with neo-orthodox theology.

When Uchimura, as a young teacher early in 1891, received the school order to "worship" the Imperial portrait, Rescript, and Signature, he had no inclination to "worship," so "bowed just slightly. Some of the professors in the school, who were opposed to Christianity, took advantage of this and began to attack him as being insolent toward the Throne. He was charged with being unpatriotic, a rebel, disloyal, etc., and was at last forced to resign his position."[10]

The bitter attack that fell upon him sent him to his sickbed where friends came to urge him to change his view. He agreed to make an apology for patriotic reasons and sent a friend to be his representative in bowing before the Rescript. When Uemura heard of this sad fall, he wrote in his *Gospel Witness*, "We are Protestants. We dare not worship even a portrait of Christ the King of Kings lest it be said that we worship the form of a man. We do not bow in worship even to the Bible which was revealed by God, lest we sin against what is written in this Book. Therefore, are we going to fall down and worship this Rescript?"[11] Excessive nationalism was Uchimura's pitfall. Later he was to write, "I love two J's and no third; one is Jesus and the other is Japan. I do not know which I love more, Jesus or Japan."[12]

The Rescript at first caused a great stir in Christian circles, and real opposition to the demands of the Ministry of Education by evangelical missionaries and Japanese Christians arose. Yet gradually resistance declined and the government's instructions were accepted. One Japanese Christian historian gave this explanation: "Fortunately the Minister of Education published an official statement concerning the Imperial Rescript, saying that to worship does not mean anything religious but only 'to pay homage' to the gracious ruler himself according to social custom. It proved to be expedient that this statement was published at this juncture. The protest of the Christians came to an end in a short time, for they were satisfied by the official statement."[13] The pressure of fear that there was no way other than acceptance by which to keep the Christian schools open, or to enable the children of Christians to receive the free education of the government schools, certainly was a major contributing factor.

In 1900, the government made it still easier for Christians to argue that the Rescript ceremonies could be considered outside of the religious category. That year it divided its Department of Home Affairs into a Bureau of State Shinto

Shrines and a Bureau of Religions. Since the state shrines were thus officially separated from the bureau that supervised religious matters, and since the ceremonies to reverence the emperor in the schools were also not put under the religious bureau, this gave support to those who argued that the government itself did not consider the school ceremonies to be of a religious nature. There were a great many Christians who were willing to let the pagan government decide for them as to what was religion and what was not.

Religious Nature of the Rescript Ceremonies

That the Rescript ceremonies were of a polytheistic nature, however, and therefore of a religious nature in the Christian meaning of the word, the following considerations should make clear. The very opening words of the Rescript reveal its polytheism. The "Ancestors" referred to, as the Chinese ideograph indicate, are the ancient gods of Japan, those mythological deities described in the *Kojiki*, the sacred scriptures of the Shinto faith, and the "divine emperors" descendant from them. The actual expression is *Waga Kooso Koosoo.*"

D.C. Holtom, the well-known authority on Shintoism, commenting on this, writes:

> According to the interpretation given in the commentary that accompanies the Department of Education publication, "The Fundamental Meaning of the National Structure," the meaning of the *kooso* element is: "The deities (*kamigami*), beginning with Amaterasu Omikami (the Sun Goddess), who laid the foundation of the imperial glory, and Jimmu Tenno, who established his authority over the country, spread abroad the imperial influence and was the first human Emperor." The second, or *koosoo* element, means the line of historical sovereigns from the second Emperor to the father of the reigning Emperor. We can see from this that the Rescript makes direct reference to the greatest of the Shinto deities, Amaterasu Omikami. This fact gives it the quality of a religious document. It becomes the chief sacred text of State Shinto.[14]

In addition to this, however, the Rescript declares loyalty to the emperor to be the highest motive for virtuous living. This is implicit in such phrases as the "Imperial Throne coeval with heaven and earth," and "the Way here set forth is ... infallible in all ages and true in all places." To a Christian these can be nothing but the religious concepts of a primitive polytheism. The fact that the government, from motives of policy, placed the dissemination of these doctrines in the care of the Bureau of State Shrines rather than that of the Bureau of Religions, thereby implying they were above religion (*shukyo*), does not alter the situation at all. A missionary to Japanese-occupied Manchuria, writing in 1940, has stated the issue very clearly. He wrote:

The fact that the magistrate may, by a stroke of official legerdemain, declare that ceremonies which include priesthood and altar, sacrifices and prayers, possess no religious significance, does not alter the situation in the slightest; it is not what the magistrate says about such ceremonies, but what they plainly are in themselves, that constitutes their inherent immorality and incompatibility with Christian practice. To say that the cult of the sun goddess, Amaterasu Omikami, has nothing to do with religion does not make it right for the Lord's people to participate in the worship of the sun goddess; it only means that the sin of dishonesty is added to that of idolatry. The pity is that so many are deceived by such palpable conceits, which must result in dreadful injury to their own consciences in the end.[15]

Modern altar of the descendants of the Jesuit disciples, a syncretism of Shintoism, Buddhism and Romanism, with traditional offerings of mochi (rice cakes), sake (wine) and fruit.

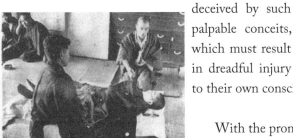

"Old Catholic" priest holds crucifix before dying youth before anointing him with "holy water."

With the promulgation of the Rescript on Education, the Shinto ideology of "the divine Emperor, divine race, and divine land" became the basic philosophy underlying the educational system. If the Christians were hesitant in reaching this conclusion, the intelligent non-Christians were able to present it and its consequences to them readily enough. In 1893, Professor Tetsujiro Inouye of Tokyo Imperial University gave some lectures entitled "The Conflict Between Education and Religion," which were widely circulated in magazine and book form, in which he demonstrated that the teachings of Christianity were in contradiction to those of the Rescript.

圖之橋本日
NIHONBASHI .

Tokyo's Nihonbashi, 1876

He stated, "Christianity advocates universalism and a love that knows no distinctions, and consequently it cannot be harmonized with the purport of the Imperial Rescript on Education which is nationalistic. Moreover, Christianity places its Heavenly Father and its Christ above the Emperor and therein it contradicts the principles of loyalty and filial piety of the Imperial Rescript on Education."[16]

Christian leaders at once counterattacked. Not a few argued that Christianity strengthened ancestor worship with its emphasis on the immortality of the soul, and that it deepened filial piety. Others, on the other hand, called attention to the emptiness of Confucian ethics when it came to matters of personal morality and purity of life. They also declared that it was in the despised universalism of Christianity, in its command to "love thy neighbor as thyself," that real patriotism lay, and not in the preachments of nationalistic fanatics who, in the name of love of country, were willing to drive it to its destruction. True patriots, they argued, while honoring their ancestors were still willing to try to correct errors of the past. This carrying the war into the opponents' camp had a good effect and the excitement subsided temporarily.

Four years later, however, some other professors of the same university took up the attack. They addressed a series of questions to the Christians. "Can the worship of His Sacred Majesty, the Emperor, which every loyal Japanese performs, be reconciled with the worship of God and Christ by Christians? Can the Japanese who is the faithful servant of Christ be regarded at the same time as the faithful servant of the Emperor and a true friend of His Majesty's faithful subjects? Or, to put it in another way, Is our Emperor to follow in the wake of Western emperors and to pray, 'Son of God, have mercy on me?'"[17]

This was followed in 1907 by one of the most carefully reasoned polemics against Christianity thus far prepared in Japan. This was a book by Dr. Hiroyuki Kato of Tokyo Imperial University entitled *Our National Structure (Kokutai) and Christianity,* in which such argumentation as this appeared:

Sovereignty in Japan is vested in a single Race-father, a form of government without peer among all the nations of the world. It is, therefore, not to be tolerated that a sovereign should be accepted who receives reverence above and beyond the Emperor and the Imperial Ancestors. Our national structure makes it impossible to permit the acceptance of a "One True God" above the Emperor. For this reason it is entirely clear that the teachings of Christianity and our national structure can never stand together.... If in the future Christianity should gradually grow in power so that the Heavenly Father should be revered more than the Emperor, greater value given to the world than to the nation, and cosmopolitanism should be esteemed more than the Japanese race—if ideas such as these should in some measure arise, I fear that loyalty and devotion as they have existed up to now would be severely weakened or destroyed.[18]

The Rescript clearly put the emperor and his deity-ancestors in the place of God, and the Christian who professed to accept its doctrine, as Kato pointed out, had either to practice deception towards the nation or to his own God. As a recent Japanese Christian historian has written, "The debate clearly proved to all concerned that the Imperial Rescript on Education was indeed the proclamation of a national anti-Christian policy. The Christians succeeded in making clear the reactionary nature of the Rescript, but at the same time the general public concluded that Christians were not loyal Japanese and turned with even greater vehemence against Christianity. The Christians were, so to speak, victorious in an argument on wrestling theory but were defeated in the ring."[19]

The bow to the imperial portrait, at the time of the Rescript reading, was likewise a religious act. One who had witnessed such a ceremony wrote, "The picture ceremony is religious worship. It cannot even be compared to prayer in a Christian church. That is, for most of the congregation, merely one of the formalities of a church service. The veneration of the imperial pictures is more comparable to the superheated emotion of an evangelistic revival."[20]

Why was this ceremony called "religious worship?" In the late 1930s, when that statement was written, the answer would probably have been, "Because of the obvious adoration and worship in the hearts and faces of the students who had been cleverly indoctrinated and fanatically excited to believe that in this 'profoundest obeisance' they were worshiping a living god himself." But if this spirit of worship was lacking, as it most probably was in the hearts of Christian students of the 1890s who performed the bow, was that bow to the portrait still an act of worship such as is forbidden to Christians?

The Biblical View of Bowing

The answer lies in the second commandment (Exodus 20:4–5), where it is declared, "Thou shalt not make unto thee any ... likeness of anything that is in heaven above, or that is in the earth beneath, or that is in the water under the earth. Thou shalt not bow down thyself to them, nor serve them." The Hebrew word translated here as "bow down" in the English, and as *ogamu* (worship) in Japanese, is *shachah*. The International Standard Bible Encyclopedia, in a learned article on the word "worship," makes it clear that the root idea of *shachah* is that of bodily prostration with a view to showing reverence. When it is performed to living men in their presence, where no idea of deity is associated, the Scriptures uniformly recognize the act of prostration or bowing as a legitimate salutation. As an act of worship to the living God, who is Spirit, or as only an act of respect in the presence of a living man, who is spirit and body, created in the image of God, *shachah* (to worship or bow down before) is correct behavior.

What the Scriptures uniformly condemn, and the second commandment specifically forbids, is the act of bowing, whether merely as an outward act or as one including the inner, emotional, worship feeling, towards anything other than living persons, specifically anything made in the "likeness of anything that is in the heaven above, or that is in the earth beneath." The act of bowing, when performed otherwise than as an act of salutation to a living person, is a worshipful act, whether performed from an inner, emotional religious feeling, or simply performed as an outward act without such feeling, according to the scriptural presentation of the matter.

The three young Hebrew heroes of the third chapter of Daniel obviously so understood it, for if the only *shachah* (bow down or worship) forbidden by the second commandment was one associated with an inner religious feeling, then they could have bowed down in good conscience knowing that there was no such feeling in their hearts. They well knew, however, that it was the act of bowing itself which was forbidden and that to do so would be to "worship the image." Thus apart from the fact that the school bow to the portrait was made to the picture of one who was declared to be a god, and that the bow required was for the students' "profoundest obeisance," of which there could be none deeper in act or inner meaning, apart from these obvious considerations, the fact that the bow was to the material reproduction of a man should have been enough for Christians to classify it in the category of forbidden acts of an idolatrous nature. That they did not do so established the practice of compromise with the national polytheism for three generations of Christians to come, leaving an imprint so deep that even today few churches in Japan have completely extracted themselves from it. This early failure to discern between that which could be rendered "to Caesar" and that which was God's alone resulted in the planting of a seed which within a half-century was to bring forth a harvest of destruction in the moral fiber of the church.

The willingness of the Christian forces to accept the government's interpretation and do the required obeisance, along with their failure to unite in forthright protest against it, was perhaps the most tragic failure in the history of Christianity in Japan. A united decision to the effect that they would not conduct such ceremonies in Christian schools, nor approve children of Christians participating in them in government schools, even to the extent of closing the Christian schools on the ceremony days, or keeping their children home from government schools, regardless of the consequences, might well have prevailed with the government. It would have at least put real backbone into the church and set a precedent of no compromise with polytheism. The course chosen, however, had the opposite effect.

The value of such representations to the government, and letters to the public press on such issues, was clearly revealed at the turn of the century. At that time the Ministry of Education issued an Imperial Ordinance prohibiting schools from accepting children of grade school age if such schools did not have a government license. It was declared as necessary for the obtaining of such a license that no religious instruction, either on a compulsory or voluntary basis, be given. This time a large majority of Christian educators, and denominations in such work, made united representations to the government officials, and to the newspapers, with the result that, within a short time, special concessions were made. Within four years such other concessions were granted as to allow Christian schools completely to circumvent the original intent of the prohibition.

The victories won for the Christian cause on this point, however, by the Christian educators who refused to accept defeat, were largely empty ones, since the Christian schools had already yielded to the demand to participate in the polytheistic indoctrination of their students through the acceptance of the Rescript ceremonies. If the Christian forces of 1890 had unitedly remonstrated with the government, claiming, for instance, that the Ministry of Education was forcing the Protestant Christians to adopt the Roman Catholic practice of giving "the profoundest obeisance" to material objects; and that the ministry was forcing monotheistic Christians to participate in polytheistic indoctrination, neither of which they could possibly approve, the government might have been prevailed upon to allow exceptions for Christian schools. As it was, the Christians were led to accept a compromise with polytheism which was to have the profoundest effects on the whole course of Christianity in Japan, dooming it to failure in the future struggle with Shintoism and to an attitude of tolerance towards idolatry which still today is largely not overcome. Through the use of the Rescript on Education, and the practice of doing obeisance to the imperial portrait, polytheism was thoroughly implanted in the Christian schools of Japan. Christian children were thus indoctrinated in it, and developed a tolerant attitude toward it which was to last for decades to come.

Other Influences Undermining the Church's Pure Witness

During this early period of reaction against Christianity not only was the church led astray by those leaders who induced it to accommodate itself to the demands of Shinto ideology and polytheism in the name of patriotism, but it was also led by others into an erroneous complacency toward Buddhism, a failure to discern its essentially anti-Christian nature. Probably no single Japanese Christian had a greater effect on the thinking of Christians in this land than Kanzo Uchimura, through his prodigious writings and fame as an "independent" Christian. He frequently wrote on the subject of Christianity and Buddhism in his books and magazines, a few samples of which we can note.

"As an independent Christian," he wrote in 1915, "I thought I stood alone in this country. But now I think otherwise. Thirteen millions of my countrymen who profess the *Jodo* form of Buddhism are my brothers and sisters in faith. They take the same attitude towards their Amida Buddha that I take towards my Jesus the Christ. Change but the object of faith, and they are like me, and I am like them."[21]

Again he wrote, "It is generally thought by both Christians and Buddhists that Christianity and Buddhism are enemies to each other ... that for Christians, Christianity is the Heavenly Light while Buddhism is a sort of demon-worship, to be classed with all other superstitious beliefs.... Is Buddhism an enemy of Christianity? On the contrary, is there not the common ground upon which the two stand side by side? ... The two are essentially one in magnifying Love as the most potent power in the universe, and non-resistance as the only means to overcome evil. All other differences amount to nothing when compared with agreement as to this cardinal truth. Christianity an enemy of Buddhism? Not so!"[22]

Writing on the subject of Buddha and Christ, he said, "Buddha is the Moon; Christ is the Sun. Buddha is the Mother; Christ is the Father. Buddha is Mercy; Christ is Righteousness.... I now love the Sun more than I love the Moon; and I know that the love of the Moon is included in the love of the Sun, and that he who loves the Sun loves the Moon also."[23]

The lack of discernment necessary to describe Buddhism and Christianity as having "fundamental likeness" and "agreement" on "cardinal truth" reveals a leadership quite incapable of resisting the infiltration of Buddhist ideas into both Christian thought and practices. Among Japanese Christians, the widespread attitude of spiritual pacifism, an unwillingness to contend for the truth and expose doctrinal error undermining the faith of the church, is an illustration of the progress of the former, while the accommodation to Buddhist practices in the Christian funeral is an illustration of the latter.

The influx of modernist unbelief, through some missionaries and many students who had been sent to liberal theological schools abroad, also greatly contributed to depriving the church of the sound teaching it vitally needed to win in its life and death struggle with the empire of Shinto nationalism. As the first decade of this century progressed, modernist unbelief was increasingly circularized through publications and modernist-trained pastors. One missionary of that period was later to write:

> It is not strange that the faith of some was shaken. To many Japanese it is a recommendation for any theory that it is new. The desire of some to show their independence of former teachers made them more ready to accept strange doctrines.... Views that might have done little harm in communities that had long been instructed in Christian doctrines assumed an exaggerated importance and led men to give up apparently all their early faith.[24]

The extent of this apostasy from the Christian faith in those early decades can be seen from the following quotation made in 1920:

If we should make a list of prominent Japanese, who once converted are now apostates, their number would be found to be very large. The ranks of government officials, especially diplomats, journalists, men of letters and arts, and educationalists abound with apostate Christians. From this view-point, the propagation of Christianity has certainly been a failure. It is especially so with the intellectual and upper classes.[25]

A church, founded and taught by pastors who did not believe that the Bible spoke the sovereign voice of God Almighty, "the only infallible rule of faith and practice," men who could rationalize a defense for Christian participation in polytheistic ceremonies, could not be one prepared to follow the commands of that Bible literally, at any cost, when faced with the threat of physical persecution if it did not yield to the idolatrous demands of the polytheistic state.

Many circumstances had bent the tree the way it had grown. The deep spirit of national pride resulted in a great reluctance to resist that which was accepted as a national sentiment. This led to the failure of the early Christians to stand unitedly against the government's polytheistic indoctrination of the church's school children, with the resultant participation of the children in idolatrous practices. The "national structure" of Japan was based on polytheism, but the patriotism of pastors and teachers blinded them from facing this fact and its consequence for the Christian church. A further factor was the admiration for Buddhist thought in spite of its man-centered humanism, while the influx of modernist unbelief was certainly a terribly damaging influence. Due to all of these elements the Japanese church, in its all-important formative years, grew up in an atmosphere of compromise and accommodation certain to doom the cause of the Empire of Christ to defeat in its crucial struggle with the Shinto-militarist government of the Empire of Japan.

---

1. Kanzo Uchimura, *The Works of Uchimura*, Vol. 15, 1895. "How I Became a Christian," p. 19.

2. *Ibid.*, p. 41.

3. *Ibid.*, p. 47.

4. *Ibid.*, p. 60.

5. *Ibid.*, pp. 134-5; 137.

6. *Ibid.*, pp. 701-2.

7. *Ibid.*, p. 452.

8. C.W. Iglehart, *Cross and Crisis in Japan*, p. 53. Friendship Press, N.Y., 1957. Also *Time* magazine, April 23, 1956.

9. W.H.H. Norman, *An Interim Report on Non-Church Christianity in Japan*, 1958, Kyo Bun Kwan, Tokyo.

10. K. Aoyoshi, *op. cit.,* p. 82.

11. S.E. Boyle, "The Revival of State Shinto in Modern Japan," *The Reformation Review,* July 1954, p. 60, quoting Sekai (*The World*), February 1954, p. 47.

12. K. Uchimura, *op. cit.*, p. 599.

13. K. Aoyoshi, *op. cit.*, p. 83.

14. D.C. Holtom, *Modern Japan and Shinto Nationalism*, p. 80. University of Chicago Press, 1941.

15. J.G. Vos, "Christian Missions and the Civil Magistrate in the Far East," *Westminster Theological Journal*, Vol. III, 1940. Reprinted in pamphlet form in 1952 by JBCC, p. 8.

16. Holtom, *op. cit.*, p. 81.

17. Cary, *op. cit..* p. 97.

18. Holtom, *op. cit.*, pp. 81-2.

19. Yanagita, *op. cit.,* pp. 49-50.

20. Willard Price, *Japan and the Son of Heaven*, p. 126. Duell, Sloan and Pearce, N.Y., 1945.

21. K. Uchimura, *op. cit.,* p. 390.

22. *Ibid.*, pp. 601-2.

23. *Ibid.*, p. 577.

24. Cary, *op. cit.,* p. 94.

25. K. Uchimura, *op. cit.*, p. 352.

4

Shinto Nationalism's Shadow Falls Across the Church

"Between the early thirties and the end of the decade, Christian attitudes in Japan, both Catholic and Protestant, had changed from strong opposition to the encroachments of Shinto on their religious life to an almost equally strong effort to syncretize the two faiths."

During the first three decades of the 20th century, Christianity steadily advanced into most of the cities of Japan, into many of the towns and some of the rural communities without further major conflict with the state. Christians had apparently, for the most part, become reconciled to the idea of a "limited" compromise with the state's demands for polytheistic participation, with the hope that in this way freedom to exist and expand would be continued.

There seemed little awareness of how devastating either such compromise or this indoctrination in the schools would be to the future development of the church. Thus children, who were taught the Ten Commandments in Christian Sunday schools on Sunday, were allowed to believe that there was no contradiction between the first two commandments and the polytheistic ideology of the Imperial Rescript on Education on which their school system was founded, and on which was based all their required courses of instruction on morals and ethics. Further, few of them were ever told that there was any inconsistency in giving their bow of profoundest obeisance to the Rescript and imperial portrait, or going out as a school unit to bow at the Shinto shrines (*jinja sampai*). When these same children grew up, it could hardly be expected of them that they would view the polytheism of either the state's prescribed "national spirit" (*Nippon seishin*) or the shrine worship as incompatible with Christianity, or even to look with serious disfavor upon the keeping of such symbols of polytheism as Shinto god-shelves (*kamidana*) or Buddhist altars (*Butsudan*) in their homes.

Furthermore, during these years many evangelical missionaries unconsciously fell prey to the temptation to give deference to the example of the Japanese pastors who refrained from any open conflict with the national polytheism by avoiding public preaching against Buddhism or Shintoism, or at least where followers of those religions could hear them. In this they were far behind the 17th century Jesuit missionaries who so routed the Buddhist priests in open debate that the latter refused to debate with them anymore and their followers deserted them for the new religion. The result of this silence was that the voice of the prophet was largely still in the land. A very interesting comment on this matter has been made by one of Japan's most famous Christian university professors, when he was asked why Japanese Christians had not taken up a more forthright opposition against the nationalism and polytheism that led to the war. "One reason was the missionaries," Professor Yanaihara replied.

> They came into a strange culture and had to make their message winsome and attractive. Etiquette demanded that they not be too outspoken in criticizing life around them. The result was that they produced a church which never offended anything or anybody. It was too genteel, too gracious, too amiable, too susceptible to flattery. It had no backbone. It was never the church militant, and it should have been. Also the missionaries tended to emphasize quantity over quality, and numbers are always a handicap in focusing to a sharp point of criticism against the general social scene. The Japanese church has emphasized the social gospel to the virtual exclusion of dogmatics and the Bible. I consider this fact as significant as any in producing a church that was non-prophetic in the war years here. There was never enough Bible study in our church, never enough prophecy.[1]

By "prophecy" he was not referring to predictive prophecy but to that fearless, forthright preaching of the Word of God against sin, error, and idolatry which was the characteristic of the Old Testament prophets.

A recent comment from one who was an early missionary to Japan, serving here for over thirty years as an outstanding evangelical scholar, comes to us as a voice out of the past, and should cause real heart searching. He wrote, "I think sometimes that I made a mistake, as a missionary, in not paying more attention to Buddhism, and never preaching about it. If it was a mistake, it is one shared by almost all missionaries and by Japanese preachers as well, for you very seldom heard a word from them about Buddhism, and never an address about it intended for Buddhist believers."[2]

The following prewar quotation from a well known Japanese churchman, Dr. Akira Ebisawa, general secretary of Japan's National Christian Council before and after the war, bears out the fact that, generally speaking, only missionaries who were here in the very early days engaged in a forthright ministry against idolatry, and that, by and large, such a ministry was repudiated by the Japanese pastors.

> It may be fairly stated that the missionaries who led Christians in the Far East to break with their ancient traditions, branding them as superstitions, and to forsake ancestor worship in its entirety, were extremely narrow-minded in their views. In Japan, the destruction of the (household) Buddhist shrines (*Butsudan*) and the throwing away of the ancestral tablets (*ihai*) in the early days of Christian missions were considered to be an expression of earnest faith by missionaries of conservative and bigoted tendencies. In as much as Christianity is not a destroyer of former culture, but a fulfiller of the law and prophets, it is unfortunate that some believers are moved and controlled by fundamentalist views.

Such then was the spiritual climate in which the majority of those, who represented the Empire of Christ before the national polytheism of the Empire of Japan, lived during this century's first three decades.

Shinto Ideology and the Militarists

Toward the close of the 1920s there was a real trend in Japan in the direction of a liberal, democratic type of government, a situation that was most annoying to the Shinto-militarists. One of them, who was later to confess that it was he who, in June 1929, had arranged the dynamiting of the train of Manchurian General Chang

Tso-Lin, which caused the warlord's death, recently wrote of that period in self-defense: "The whole society was tending towards liberalism, concentrating attacks and criticism on the armed solution of the Manchurian-Monogolian problems.... But what did they think of the population problem which was increasing every year?"[4] It was just at this time that Baron Tanaka, a zealous advocate of the Shinto ideology of *hakko ichiu* (the whole world under one roof), became prime minister.

This famous phrase came from the ancient Nihonshoki, where it appears as the desire of the sun goddess's descendant, the first emperor, Jimmu, to have his rule spread over the whole world, and has since been interpreted as presenting the nation's divine destiny and duty. Tanaka's dedication to this ideology was very apparent in the memorial he presented the emperor following the Eastern Conference called by him in the summer of 1927 to discuss plans for expansion. His memorial said in part: "It seems that it was by divine will that I should assist Your Majesty to open a new era in the Far East and to develop the new constitutional empire." After outlining the plan for gaining control of Manchuria, he continued: "The Yamato Race is then embarked on the journey of world conquest."[5] He concluded by detailing the necessity of future military conquests of all of Asia and eventually the United States to fulfill the divine destiny. His thesis was thus the same as that of Lord Hotta in 1858: "The object should always be kept in view of laying a foundation for securing the hegemony over all nations."[6]

The implementation of the next step in Tanaka's plan for fulfilling *hakko ichiu* fell on a peaceful Japan suddenly, in 1931, with the invasion of Manchuria. The Shinto-militarists knew that if they were to fulfill their "divine commission," the trend toward a liberal democracy must be stopped, and that there was no more effective way to do that than war. According to the Meiji Constitution, field generals could take military action in an emergency without consulting the emperor, which provided these schemers with all the opportunity they needed, both in 1931 and 1937, of precipitating "incidents" with China that provided the emergencies and enabled them to start undeclared wars without even the emperor's knowledge. During the next ten years whenever these militarists felt their position challenged, they ruthlessly forced the opposition to yield by such acts of violence as the assassinations of 1932 and 1936 and the undeclared wars of 1931, 1937 and 1941.

As the decade drew to a close with the nation's armies bogged down on a vast front in China, the Shinto slogans of *hakko ichiu* and *seisen* (holy war) were drilled home to the people at every opportunity. The schools began using a commentary on the Ministry of Education's "Fundamental Principles of the National Structure," which taught that "the *hakko ichiu* teaching involves the purpose to extend to the four seas the imperial glory which now fills Japan itself and thereby brings in the universal reign of peace. This in turn involves the use of military power, but history shows that the military might of Japan is always that of a 'divine soldiery that is sent to bring life to all things.'"[7]

Foreign Minister Matsuoka declared in January 1940, after returning from Berlin and the signing of the Tripartite Pact, "The Manchurian Incident and the China Affair are nothing but manifestations of Japan's attempt to forestall the destruction of civilization. The Manchurian Incident should be termed the start of construction, not destruction, of world peace. The Coprosperity Sphere in the Far East is based on the spirit of *hakko ichiu*."[8]

A sample of what was said about the "holy war" can be seen in this quotation from the *Imperial News* of September 18, 1938: "No matter how much of a wrong doer, no matter how evil, a Japanese subject may have been, when once he has taken his stand on the field of battle, all his past sins are entirely atoned for and they become as nothing. The wars of Japan are carried on in the name of the Emperor and therefore they are holy wars.... Those who, with the words '*Tenno Heika Banzai*' (May the Emperor live forever) on their lips, have consummated tragic death in battle, whether they are good or whether they are bad, are thereby sanctified."[9] For them the future held the "happy expectation" of being enshrined as deities at Yasukuni Shrine and thereby joining the hosts of nation-protecting gods. Such then was the Shinto ideology that inspired the militarists to lead the nation from one war to the next, and eventual disaster.

The Church's Surrender to the Shintoist State

In the Meiji Restoration of 1868, one of the first imperial edicts promulgated by the new emperor declared, "The worship of the gods and regard for [Shinto] ceremonies are the great properties of the empire and the fundamental principles of national polity and education.... Thus the Way of the unity of religion and government (*saisei itchi*) shall be revived."[10]

Holtom, commenting on this, says, "*Sai* here means ceremony or ritual; *sei* refers to governmental or political administration; *itchi* means unity. The whole, therefore, may be translated ... 'the unity of government and Shinto ceremonies,' or the 'unity of government and religion.'"

In this avowed unity between the empire of Japan and the Shinto religion lay all the potential for a rugged conflict between Christian church and Shinto state, whenever the church had courage and discernment enough to use its God-given freedom of conscience to teach noncompliance with the state's demands for participation in polytheistic practices. The Meiji Constitution's guarantee of freedom of religion was limited to those not opposing the "national structure" based on the Shinto ideology. The actual statement in the Constitution read: "Japanese subjects shall, within limits not prejudical to peace and order, and not antagonistic to their duties as subjects, enjoy freedom of religious belief."[12]

The trouble was that the phrase "their duties as subjects" was interpreted to mean support of the "national polity" mentioned in the Imperial Rescript on Education, and therefore it was said that the Constitution did not grant freedom to oppose the Rescript's Shintoist doctrine of the divine emperor, divine land, and divine people, nor to refuse to participate in ceremonies stemming from these beliefs, when such were ordered. A Christian, when faced with the problem of whether to obey or not, had to choose one of two alternatives. He could compromise his Christian principles and participate in the required polytheistic practices, thereby denying the Lord whom he professed, or he could dare to be a Daniel, or a Peter, and say, "We must obey God rather than man." In the latter case, the Constitution could be interpreted as giving him no protection and he was open to the charge of lese majesty as well as the epithet *hikokumin*, a despiser of the nation. The reason that there were few Christians against whom such charges were hurled was due to the fact that there were few who chose this latter course.

In the liberal days prior to 1931, Christian groups had not hesitated to declare that Shinto Shrine ceremonies were religious and that government statements to the contrary were unreasonable. For instance, in 1917 the Federated Churches of Japan, a Protestant council, had declared, "To lead the people into a vague religious exercise under the pretext of reverence towards ancestors, and thus to mix the two things, is not only irrational, but results in harm to education and hinders in many ways the progress of the people."[13] In 1930, the National Christian Council of Japan issued a statement which said in part, "To treat the Shinto shrines, which from of old have been religious, as nonreligious has been unreasonable. The shrines of Shrine (State) Shinto are actually engaged in religious functions. This has given rise to much confusion. Furthermore, recently the Government in its effort to foster religious faith has promoted worship at the shrines of Shrine Shinto and even made it compulsory. This is clearly contrary to the policy that Shrine Shinto is nonreligious."[14]

In spite of these plain statements, in 1936 the NCC did a right about-face and declared, "We accept the definition of the government that the Shinto shrine is nonreligious."[15]

Since during those six years nothing had changed in Shintoism, it was obvious something had in the NCC. Under the short span of the Shinto-military dictatorship, sufficient pressure had been brought to bear to cause the Christians to realize that nonpersecution could only be expected if they would agree to participate in the required Shinto rites. Church members who throughout their school days had repeated the Rescript on Education, bowed to the imperial portrait, and gone out to the Shinto shrines to do obeisance were not prepared to resist the state on this issue.

After the war, in 1949, the NCC representatives, without any apology, frankly stated in their report to the Far Eastern delegates of the World Council of Churches' Bangkok conference: "There seemed only two alternatives for the church to follow, either to clash with the militaristic regime at the expense of complete dissolution of the churches and even martyrdom, or to suffer together with their fellow countrymen in perseverance and sacrifice. The sense of national solidarity led our church people to choose the latter position."[16]

The Roman Catholics likewise were ready to sacrifice their principles to save their physical organization. Previously, in 1918, the Bishop of Nagasaki proclaimed, "Shrine worship ... is an organized form of reverence to supernatural beings and must be regarded as religion. Moreover, it is a religion forced upon the people.... We regret exceedingly that as Catholics we cannot accept the interpretation of shrine worship given by the government, nor can we visit the shrines and engage in the services for the dead, nor can we ever pay respects to the so-called gods."[17] In 1931, a Japanese bishop stated, "The Shinto shrines, so the high authorities of the government tell us, do not maintain a religion, but as a matter of fact the ceremonies that are performed therein have a full religious character ... [yet] students are forced to go to the shrines and are punished if they refuse."[19]

In spite of these forthright statements before the days of the military dictatorship, on May 25, 1936, the Office of the Sacred Congregation on Propaganda Fide at Rome reversed this position and declared that, "Since (Shrine) ceremonies of this kind are endowed with a purely civil value, it is lawful for Catholics to join in them."[19]

Baker points out that, "Between the early thirties and the end of the decade, Christian attitudes in Japan, both Catholic and Protestant, had changed from strong opposition to the encroachments of Shinto on their religious life to an almost equally strong effort to syncretize the two faiths."[20] The Shinto militarists had done their work well. Through a half-century of indoctrination of the nation's youth in Shinto ideology, and the belief that patriotism involved subscription to it, that which represented the Empire of Christ was ready and willing to offer to the Empire of Japan what rightfully it could give to God alone.

---

1. Richard T. Baker, *Darkness of the Sun*, pp. 167-8. Abingdon-Cokesbury Press, New York, 1947.

2. Albertus Pieters, in a letter to a missionary in Japan, in 1954.

3. A. Ebisawa, "Korean Christianity, Its Problems and Current Developments," *Contemporary Japan*, December 1938.

4. D. Kawamoto, *Japan Digest*, January 1955, p. 37.

5. Published by the World Peace Movement in the *China Critic*, September 1931.

6. H Satoh, *op. cit.*

7. Holtom, *op. cit.*, p. 23.

8. O.T. Tolischus, *Tokyo Record*, p. 30. Reynal & Hitchcock, New York, 1943.

9. Holtom, *op. cit.*, p. 44.

10. *Ibid.*

11. *Ibid*, p. 4.

12. Cary, *op. cit.*, p. 94.

13. Holtom, *op. cit.*, p. 96.

14. Mid, p. 97.

15. Holtom, *op. cit.*, p. 97.

16. Mimeographed report presented to the conference at Bangkok in 1949.

17. Holtom, *op. cit.*, p. 98.

18. *Ibid.*, p. 98.

19. *Ibid.*, p. 99.

20. Baker, *op. cit.*, p. 67.

5

Some Christians Who Resisted

The Lord always raises up a faithful witness to Himself, and in each of the lands in which this struggle between the Empire of Japan and that of Christ was being waged this became apparent. The first Christian group to come into head-on conflict with the authorities of the state—because of their uncompromising refusal to participate in the required Shinto ceremonies—was one in Ogaki, Gifu Ken, members of a church of the Mino Mission. The crisis came in 1933 when one of the Sunday school boys stated to his government school teacher that he could not go with the class on their expedition to the Grand Shrine of Ise, some fifty miles distant, to worship the sun goddess. This 12-year-old boy, with his 11-year-old brother, stated clearly that they were Christians and could not participate in such idolatry. Their mother was summoned to the school and when she supported the position of the boys the police were called.

Police and detectives then called on the missionaries and when they endorsed the stand of the Christian family the battle was on. When later they left, still in great wrath, Miss Weidner, head of the mission, called a prayer meeting with the statement, "This is a matter of life and death: Ise Shrine has been touched. We may be killed at any moment!" That Sunday night the street meeting was broken up by an angry mob and stones were thrown at the group, while later a large crowd gathered outside the mission entrance to call out imprecations.

One man shouted, "You say the God of heaven helps, but He is not helping you folks," and the crowd laughed. But God stayed the hands of the mob from doing them harm. The God of heaven, who is a God of mercy as well as justice, was to give the nation a few more years in which to turn back from its tragic course of following the Shinto-militarists before He was to rend the government from the Shintoist control, reveal the helplessness of the Shinto gods, and open the doors of the nation to the free preaching of the gospel of Christ everywhere. Meanwhile, He used the fear of international repercussions to move the police to stay the hands of the angry mob from further acts of violence.

To get some realization of the magnitude of the offense in the eyes of the authorities of a school boy's refusal to do obeisance before the Grand Shrine of Ise, the following quotation from a 1931 school textbook of a required ethics course should be noted:

> Inasmuch as Amaterasu-Omikami is the Ancestress of the Emperor, she is the most venerated deity in our land of Japan. And since the Grand Imperial Shrine is the sanctuary where this Great Deity is worshipped, those who are Japanese, in addition to being obedient to the Emperor, must always revere and honor this shrine. You children should also await a suitable opportunity for making pilgrimage to the Grand Imperial Shrine, and, in addition to gaining an understanding of the majesty of the national structure (*kokutai*), should pray for the prosperity of the Imperial Family.

The turmoil stirred up by the refusal of these Christians in Ogaki to worship the goddess of Ise spread to the front pages of the newspapers throughout the nation. One of the missionaries later wrote:

> Meetings against the Mino Mission were held for ten nights in succession in the various Buddhist temples of the town. Large posters were displayed throughout

the city, which read, "In order to protect the National Structure of Japan let us stand against the Mino Mission." Newspapers took up the issue and scores of articles were written against us.… The greatest newspaper in all Japan sought to warn the people of our "dangerous" doctrine in writing up Miss Weidner's interview with the Minister of Education in Tokyo. Large headlines read, "The Mino Mission refuses to recognize any other god than the God of the Bible." We read it and said, "Praise the Lord." We could not have paid for such advertising![1]

It is interesting to note that the Minister of Education referred to above was none other than the postwar prime minister, Hatoyama.

The published report of one of the missionaries stated that frequently the authorities "did their best to convince us that obeisance at the shrines was only patriotism; but when they found their efforts useless, the detectives themselves admitted that it actually was worship. But even so, said they, the Mission must compromise. Miss Weidner replied, 'we will never compromise!'"[2]

Shintoism provides no absolute standards of good and evil, right and wrong, truth and error. The expression *uso mo hoben* ("a lie is a convenience") is a common philosophical outlook. Thus, that Christians should be willing to lay down their lives rather than do "wrong" by compromising a point of their religious convictions was quite incredible." To avoid trouble, don't oppose this thing," they were told, in keeping with their proverb, *Nagai mono niwa makarero*, meaning that one should not resist that which is more powerful.

To Obey the Emperor is Man's Summum Bonum

The nearest the required ethics courses in the government schools came to an absolute moral standard was the teaching that the emperor, as a living god, was infallible; he could do no wrong. Thus "good," man's *summum bonum*, was to serve him; "right" was always to follow his instructions with implicit obedience; and "truth" was what he said, although all he could ever say officially was what the Shinto-militarists wrote out for him to declare. The proof to them that this was a sufficient moral standard was the fact that it always worked; following the instructions which were issued through the emperor had led from one spectacular success to another. Shintoism's lack of providing any absolute standards for moral conduct led inevitably to the standard of "success" becoming the one by which all things were judged. This lack led to a tendency readily to switch from one conviction to another, or even from one supreme loyalty to another. A recent comment on this tendency is worth quoting.

> The roots of this attitude could be found in an old and often quoted Japanese proverb. "*Kateba kangun; makereba zokugun,*" it runs, "The Emperor's army if you win; the rebel army—if you lose." Nothing could better epitomize the Japanese ethical system; its pragmatic worship of pure success, its substitution of a maze of contractual obligations for a definite notion of good and evil.[3]

All of this had its bearing on the Ogaki case in 1933. When faced with the adamant stand of the Christians, the people and the authorities did what those dominated by Shinto ideology have usually done when faced with a situation they found they were powerless to change—they gave up trying to resist it! To continue quoting from the missionary report mentioned above:

> The persecution finally died down and we went about unmolested. In fact, after the war broke out with China (1937), when many missions were not permitted to have street meetings, we held meetings on the street without any interference. Police and detectives had come to recognize, and even respect, the uncompromising stand of the Mino Mission. We missionaries were not put out of Japan in spite of our stand against Emperor-worship in its entirety, which includes bowing before the Emperor's portrait and toward Tokyo. This latter idolatrous act is known as *Kyujoyohai* and means "worshipping the Imperial Palace from afar."[4]

The tragedy was that in spite of this uncompromising stand taken for the true Christian faith before the whole nation, no other Christian group publicly came to the support of those who made it, even to declare that their position on shrine obeisance was the only consistent one for Christians to take. Some groups sent observers to bring back a report on the situation, but these all declared, "Don't touch it! It's dangerous." Yet what a wonderful opportunity it did present for united evangelical action for a united Christian voice raised throughout the nation to declare that the church's highest allegiance was to her Lord, and that her confession must ever be, "We must obey God rather than man." Had such a united testimony been raised then, with resolute refusal to yield this principle, the whole situation might have changed and the Pacific War might never have become a reality.

The heart of the problem in evangelical circles in those days, was not that pastors or Christian workers were ordered to do shrine worship or *yohai* in their churches, for those orders came later, but that these Christian leaders allowed their children to go out with the other school children to do them. Parents who did this were in no position to condemn it, but rather had to defend it; and the children who had done it in school days saw no reason for resisting it as adults. Apart from this one mission and some individual missionaries, none took the position that a pastor or church worker who allowed his children to do *jinja sampai* could not continue in his position. It was the lack of discernment on this all-important matter of the indoctrination of the church's children, stemming far back to the compromise on the matter of the Rescript ceremonies, which brought about the undoing of the cause of Christ in the struggle with the Shinto Empire.

As the decade of the 1930s progressed, the pressure of the Shinto nationalists, who were in full control in the government, did not diminish but only increased on the nation and the church. One who was in Japan as a teacher of English later described some of the events revealing the intensification of the grip of Shinto fanaticism upon the people.[5] Whereas originally the Imperial Rescript on Education could be read from a book, held in bare hands, by the late thirties it had to be read from a scroll and held in hands clothed with fresh, white gloves. Schools had to have special safes for the repose of the scroll and the imperial portraits. After one school principal committed suicide because the portraits were destroyed when the school burned down, other schools had special buidings constructed on the grounds for the safe holding of the portrait and scroll. Children of mission schools were ordered along with the other school children to make regular expeditions to the state Shinto shrines and do obeisance before them. In a mission school in Sendai, each time the Rescript was read the stained glass picture of Christ had to be covered with a curtain so that the Lord could not look down on the holy Rescript and the picture of the divine emperor! Orders were even issued against having a Bible in a classroom for any reason, as it was declared to be "detrimental to the moral education of the Japanese."

The writer returned to Japan in the summer of 1938, on his way to Manchukuo (Manchuria), and that August at missionary prayer meetings in Karuizawa sensed a tenseness and foreboding in the air. Prayers were made for holy boldness, but little of such was to be displayed. The churches in Japan had apparently made up their minds that they would accommodate themselves to the state on the shrine issue.

The Conflict with Shinto Ideology in Korea

The reports coming from Korea, however, were quite different. There, outstanding Christian leaders were already in prison for their opposition to Christians doing shrine obeisance, and all knew that the next meeting of the Presbyterian General Assembly in Pyang Yang (Heijo) would be a critical one. The story was being told of how Governor General Minami of Korea (executed by the War Crimes Court of the Allied Powers after the war), while riding by train that year past the great Presbyterian Mission compound of high school, college, seminary, hospital, and mission-home buildings, had remarked, "All of this must come under our control if we are truly to rule here."

For some time a concentrated effort had been made in Korea to bring the church under the control of the Shinto government, with participation in its polytheistic worship. A missionary to Korea has given a penetrating analysis of the situation of those days.

From 1910 to 1931 there was constant pressure, especially in the schools, to bow to the Emperor's picture, to attend special ceremonies at shrines, to offer prayers to the dead, and to bow towards the Emperor's palace. The Christian leaders in some denominations were successful in withstanding it, but in others they gave in. But even in this period there was a breaking down of resistance in some respects. First, some missions and schools made no issue of the matter with missionaries, native pastors and school teachers bowing before the Shinto shrines. Thus the testimony of the Christians was not united on the subject.

Second, because in the eyes of the world "recognized schools" (i.e., those obtaining official government recognition by eliminating all Christian instruction from their curricula) had a better standing than the non-recognized "designated schools" (i.e. those refusing "recognition" in order to continue Christian instruction, but "designated" as schools teaching an equivalent education), many worldly "Christians" coveted this superior "standing" for their children. If their own denominational schools opposed shrine worship, and were therefore in the unrecognized class, they frequently sent their children to those "recognized"

Christian schools where shrine worship was practiced, thereby compromising their consciences and committing themselves and their children to the position that shrine worship was not sinful idolatry. Third, pastors who vigorously opposed shrine worship in their own denominational high schools allowed their children to go to government grade schools where they bowed with the other children and naturally were indoctrinated with the idea that there was no wrong in such an act. Missionaries and pastors approved discipline for parents who married their children to non-Christians yet did not discipline parents who wilfully sent their children to schools where they were compelled to worship at shrines.

During the 1930s, the Shinto government pushed the shrine issue until shrine worship was declared compulsory for *all* schools, "designated" as well as "recognized." At first there was a certain freedom to discuss these things. Time after time committees of the missions were sent to present the Christian side of the matter to the Governor General, and even to Cabinet ministers in Japan.... The government, however, insisted that shrine worship was purely patriotic and not religious, even though it was pointed out that shrine *(jinja)* means "spirit house," that prayers were offered there to the dead, and that spirits of the dead were said to come and go there.... The government also stated that the schools were established under the Imperial Rescript on Education which declared that the object of education was to make good citizens. To be a good citizen one had to do *jinja sampai* (shrine worship), so schools under the Rescript (i.e., all of them) must go to the shrines, they reasoned.

At about this time, the government began to refuse to let even mission groups meet if they were to discuss the shrine issue. They were told that even to mention it would be considered lese majesty. Christian ministers and laymen who spoke against shrine worship were imprisoned in great numbers. Mission schools were ordered to go out to bow to the shrines and argument was no longer tolerated. The Southern Presbyterian Mission closed its schools outright rather than participate in shrine ceremonies. The Northern Presbyterian Mission was handicapped by a minority of influential missionaries who saw no great harm in shrine worship, together with the fact that the modernist influenced Mission Board in New York had no strong convictions against it.... The minority in the Mission, with the Home Board's backing, put through a deal whereby many schools were transferred to Korean hands. By this act the Mission could say to its home constituency that it had no responsibility in shrine bowing, and also it avoided trouble with those Koreans who did not want to see the schools closed. In effect, however, this turned schools, built with Christian money, over to shrine worship, as no Korean group was strong enough to stand against the government pressure on an issue which missionaries, with a certain amount of immunity as foreigners, were not able wholly to resist.

As the shrine issue was being settled to the satisfaction of the authorities in the schools, they began to concentrate on enforcing the bow on the Church as well. Forgotten was the issue of bowing to the flag, or the oft-repeated statement that it was only in the realm of secular education that shrine worship was necessary for building good citizens.... Some of the strongest men in the Church were imprisoned while others were muzzled from fear of the consequences of breaking the law forbidding any discussion of the shrine issue. The few missionaries, and others, who favored approving the shrine bow were given a good deal of publicity in the government-controlled public press, but any news of individuals or groups who made strong protests, or who were imprisoned for their testimony on this issue, as many were, was pretty well kept out of the press to give the impression that the Church was gradually accepting the bow.

Christians imprisoned often appealed to the fact that the laws of the Church forbade shrine worship, seeking to hide behind the strength of numbers. The authorities determined in 1939, however, to get an action passed through the General Assembly favoring shrine worship to remove this excuse from them.... Orders were issued from the capital for the police to interrogate the commissioners to the Assembly in their respective communities. Thus they were made to face the issue of where they stood on the shrine issue singly, and in their own localities where refusal to comply with the state's position could subject them to the numerous aggravations possible in a police state, or imprisonment itself. By refusing travel permission to those who were outspoken against bowing, the authorities arranged it so that only those commissioners who would vote for shrine worship, or who would pledge to keep silence on the subject at the Assembly, were allowed to go.[6]

The Assembly was attended by more than one hundred policemen, about half in plain clothes, who sought to listen to every conversation. Missionary commissioners who would not promise to be silent when the issue came up were refused a voice on the floor by a moderator who was under the power of the authorities. The motion submitted read, "Resolved that obeisance at Shinto shrines (*jinja sampai*) is not a religious act and is not in conflict with Christian teaching, It should be performed as a matter of first importance thus maintaining a patriotic zeal." An affirmative vote was called for and given cattered assent, but no negative vote was called. In this manner the Presbyterian Church gave its approval to shrine worship.[7] The Methodist bishop had already gone out to the shrine to bow, as had the representatives of the Holiness Church in Korea and the Seventh Day Adventist Church. The Vatican had also earlier complied, reversing the position of the priests on the field.

Church leaders in Japan were asked to use their influence, and gladly did so, to make all this more palatable to the Korean Christians. Dr. Kagawa was given an expense-free lecture tour of Korea and Manchukuo, by the government-owned South Manchurian Railway, to urge the Christians to accept the required shrine worship. Dr. A. Ebisawa, General Secretary of Japan's NCC, contributed the article on "Korean Christianity—Its Problems and Current Development" mentioned earlier. He wrote as follows:

A print of early railway transportation in Tokyo

In Japan proper the question of the relationship between Christianity and the shrine is practically a settled one…. This attitude [that shrine obeisance is nonreligious in nature] is generally accepted by Japanese Christians…. On the other hand, demanding shrine worship in Korea for the manifestation of national consciousness, under Japanese rule, had created a complicated situation. The missionaries, who had taught Korean Christians to destroy, root and branch, the *Sunhandong*, the shrines for ancestral worship existing in villages from ancient times, as superstitions, could not now cause them in any wise to worship at shrines of a similar nature. It may be fairly stated that the missionaries who led Christians in the East to break with their ancient traditions, branding them as superstitions, and to forsake the custom of ancestor worship in its entirety were extremely narrow minded in their views.[8]

Once the church had given in on the shrine issue the Shinto government pressed for more. The same General Assembly that approved the bow was persuaded also to vote agreement to register themselves under the earlier promulgated Law to Control the Religious Propagator and Institution. Similar laws had also been promulgated in Taiwan, Manchukuo and Japan. The Chinese ideograph used for the word "control" was a strong one, formed from the component parts of an outstretched hand reaching for an ear, a rather graphic picture of the kind of control the Shinto state desired to obtain over the Christian church through this law. One forthright missionary, describing the compromise with apostasy with which The Foreign Missions Conference of North America became involved by their endorsement of the various united churches in the Japanese empire, churches that submitted to this law and shrine worship, summarized this law as one "which utterly destroyed religious liberty, reduced the church to bondage to the totalitarian state, and required churches and preachers to apply for and obtain licenses from the State, thereby making the very existence of the church as a religious body contingent upon express permission of government officials, and virtually recognizing the Emperor as the head of the church. Quite a number of things, including preaching against 'local customs,' are forbidden by this ordinance under penalty of fine, imprisonment, or revocation of license."[9]

Agreement to register under this law was of course an agreement to abide by its tenets, thereby accepting the supervision of the state not only in innocent civil matters but in spiritual matters also. This involved even what the church must teach (i.e., shrine worship as "the duty of national subjects") and what it must not teach (i.e., any doctrine "counter to the duties of the people" or their "local customs"). Serious consideration of this law revealed that there was no way one could register under its provisions without compromising Christian principles.

The Korea missionary declared in his lecture:

The government used the religious control law to amalgamate all the denominations into a government-controlled, government-serving church. The church was forbidden to read certain parts of the Scriptures and to sing certain hymns. Shrine worship, bowing to the flag and to the east (*kyujo yohai*) were made compulsory in the church and the latter at least at all worship services. Small shrines (*kamidana*) were then installed in the churches. Non-cooperating ministers were imprisoned, several tens dying there; church groups which did not cooperate were dissolved, or, what amounted to the same thing, arbitrarily amalgamated with groups that would cooperate.[10]

All of these steps were accomplished within four years from the time the assembly voted to approve shrine worship!

Some Heroes of the Faith in Manchukuo

Not only in Korea, but in Manchukuo also, there were Christians who refused to compromise on this issue, some suffering imprisonment and death for the Word of God and the testimony of Jesus Christ. During these years many Korean Christians had fled the threat of persecution in Korea and gone up to Manchukuo. Following the capitulation of the assembly, those living in the Harbin area renounced the assembly's jurisdiction and formed their own independent Presbyterian church, working with Bruce Hunt who had withdrawn from the Northern Presbyterian Church and joined the Orthodox Presbyterian body. This group compiled a seven-page document of Scripture teaching on idolatry and solemnly covenanted together that they would never participate in Shinto worship ceremonies nor allow their children to go to schools where such was done. That summer, June 1940, this church was suddenly denounced in a front-page news story entitled, "Secret Death Pact Organization Against Shrine Worship and Japanese Education Uncovered!" A correspondent for a Methodist periodical, in Korea after the war, described this group as one which "put up one of the strongest shows of resistance, gloried in deaths as martyrs, and took their sons out of schools rather than have them receive a Babylonian education. For all this they were persecuted…. At least three were killed."[11] It was the present writer's privilege to have known and had fellowship with those three.

Evangelist Kim

The first was Evangelist Kim who came to Harbin from North Korea and early in 1940 began attending one of Mr. Hunt's services, although refusing to take active part. Finally, one day he came to tell the missionary his story. As an evangelist in Korea who had been vociferous against shrine worship, he had been arrested, tortured and released a series of eight times. The thought-police, in an effort at first to get him to be silent on the shrine issue and then later to agree that it was all right for Christians to perform shrine worship, had kept after him until he had broken. The last time, as he was being given the infamous "water cure," stretched out on a bench with his head hanging down, while water was poured from a kettle down his nostrils, near to the point of strangulation and in frantic despair, he had finally agreed to put his seal to a paper declaring his approval of Shinto shrine worship. Such were the means by which Shintoism was propagated in the interests of *hakko ichiu*!

When Kim had been released and realized what he had done, his soul was flooded with remorse. He gave up his work and fled to Manchukuo to get away from it all. But the Lord led him right to one of the few groups in that vast land who were standing for the same things he had stood! Now he had determined that he could no longer let this thing rest on his conscience. He had come to the missionary to confess it and to say he felt that he must write back to the police station in Korea to tell them that he had lied under torture and that he did not really approve of shrine worship. He knew full well that this would mean re-arrest but he felt that he must do it. Within a short time two special police arrived to imprison him for the ninth time.

Through that spring and hot summer he was kept in a small cement cell until he was unable to stand from weakness due to dysentery and malnutrition. Finally in November, thinking that he was on the point of death, the police called a friend to come and get him before he should die in the prison. He was laid out on the frozen ground for an hour before his friend could get there to take him to the little dispensary operated by Dr. and Mrs. Roy Byram, missionaries of the Independent Board for Presbyterian Foreign Missions. There he gradually regained strength until he could go home with the use of crutches. That winter he was forbidden to leave his house, but Koreans came from many places to hear his quiet, radiant and un-complaining testimony for the Lord. The next spring he was rearrested, this time not again to be released until the rigors of prison life had taken their toll and he was given the release of death in 1943. Yet we know that this was not death but an entrance into glory. The last word to be heard of him came from fellow prisoners who testified that his saintly and godly life had made a tremendous impression on his captors. Of such heroes of the faith was it written, "Of whom the world was not worthy."

Sunday School Teacher, Miss An

The second of these three heroes was a young woman, a Sunday school teacher, Miss An. Her friend, a Bible woman, had been arrested shortly after Evangelist Kim, in the spring of 1940, and because Miss An had once worked for an officer in the police station, she went to him to seek his help in obtaining the Bible woman's release. Instead, for a week she was daily interrogated and bravely gave her testimony to the fact that she would not compromise with Shintoism. After a week of this she too was imprisoned. By November, she was at the point of death and like Kim was released and brought to the dispensary. The next morning the author went to call on her, and found but little by which she could still be recognized. The happy, healthy young woman was only skin and bones, and green with jaundice. A few days later, as Dr. Byram entered her room, he saw her suddenly sit up and exclaim, "I go into the presence of my Father." At that very moment she died, a Christian martyr who had sealed her testimony with her life, faithful to the end.

Miss An, martyr for the faith in Harbin

Evangelist Ni

The third hero of the faith was a country evangelist, like the other two, a noble Christian. Having spent ten days out in the country with Mr. Ni, in the fall of 1940 on an evangelistic tour, the writer came to appreciate what a wonderful man of God he was. We visited some of his groups and one of the secret schools where these covenanted Christians were educating their children. During the spring of 1941 he was arrested and before the war was over he too had resisted compromise unto death.

In the fall of 1941 many others were arrested and finally, on October 22, Mr. Bruce Hunt of the Orthodox Presbyterian Mission and Dr. and Mrs. Roy Byram of the Independent Board for Presbyterian Foreign Missions were also incarcerated. They were taken south to the Korean border and there questioned intensely for a number of days. There they were charged with propagating a religion which was diametrically opposed to state Shinto and of maintaining that Jehovah God and not the sun goddess was the true God and Savior. The trial was held before Japanese judges and military officers and consisted of more long hours of questioning. This time, however, it was about what the Bible taught concerning God, Christ's kingdom, the future return of Christ, and the place of the nations, and Japan, then. Would Japanese emperors, too, have to recognize Christ as Lord of all at His return? Finally the verdict was given: "Judgment deferred for two years."

Mrs. Byram later wrote, "Immediately the Koreans in the courtroom began to ex-

The emperor on his white horse at the Yoyogi Parade Grounds (Washington Heights), 1934

claim, '*Choi upso, choi upso,*' which means literally 'Crime is lacking,' that is, 'They are not pronounced guilty.' What a triumph! ... But who will render that judgment?"[12]

Before the two years were up, the folly of the Shinto faith and dreams was coming to light. On the night of December 5, they were brought before the provincial governor and told that "the religion they taught could not be tolerated in that land. By teaching there is but One True God, Who alone has the right to the worship of all races of mankind, they would undermine the very foundations on which the Empire rested." Mrs. Byram went on to say, "Perhaps the most significant statement made that night was that not Jehovah but Amaterasu-Omi-Kami was the God of their land and that all the world was soon to know it. This was less than two days before Pearl Harbor. Did the governor himself know how near the day of trial was?"[13] A bitter winter's imprisonment, however, lay ahead of the faithful missionaries before they were to be repatriated.

There were faithful ones who refused to compromise on the shrine and "Religious Control Law" issues among Korean Christians in Manchukuo and also Chinese. A missionary who made a keen analysis of that law, and took an active part in opposing it, later wrote, "Perhaps 4 or 5% of the missionaries said, 'It is wrong in principle,' and refused to sign up or comply with the law in any way. The other 95% were also divided among themselves.... Some said, 'We will comply with this demand, more or less against our conscience and better judgment, in order to keep the door open for preaching the Gospel; but when the officials come around with another demand asking us to worship at the shrines, then we will refuse to comply.' When the deadline came, about 95% of the churches, missionaries and native Christian leaders complied and signed up."[14]

This meant that in order to exist and carry on their work they were willing to agree not to teach anything against the idolatrous customs of the land that were plaguing the church. Quite different was this approach of preaching a "limited gospel" in order to escape trouble, from that of Paul who testified to the Ephesian elders, "Wherefore I take you to record this day, that I am pure from the blood of all men; for I have not shunned to declare unto you all the counsel of God" (Acts 20:26–27).

In speaking further of Covenanter churches in the Tsitsihar area, Mr. Vos wrote:

> Although the compromising churches freely predicted our early liquidation God greatly blessed our testimony, and up to the time when our last Covenanter missionaries were repatriated (summer 1942) our Covenanter churches in Manchuria (Manchukuo), with one exception, were still open and preaching the Gospel in spite of the wrath of the authorities. (The one exception was a church which disbanded entirely, rather than submit to being closed by the government, or forced into the united church.) I mean these churches were open and carrying on without having compromised or acted against conscience. This rather irritated some of the compromisers (perhaps their consciences hurt them some) and in the end it had a rather humorous result. When the Japanese authorities sent orders to all churches to put a Shinto shrine in the church buildings and to start worshipping it by April 1, 1943, the Covenanter Churches, being regarded as legally non-existent, did not get any orders to do these things, while those who held government licenses got their orders![15]

Here was a vindication of the truth of the words of the man of God in 1 Samuel 2:30, "for them that honour me I will honour, and they that despise me shall be lightly esteemed." Through those critical years we can see what is oft revealed in church history in times of crisis, that through those who have the spiritual discernment to see the issues, and the faith to maintain the integrity of God uncompromised, our God has a vivid testimony of His truth to give to the nations.

One of the brightest stories of resistance came out of the city of Peking. Pastor Wang Ming-Tao was an ardent fundamentalist and the beloved pastor of Peking's best attended church. It was a large independent church, filled to capacity every Sunday. When the wartime regulation was announced requiring the Protestant churches of China to unite, Wang Ming-Tao knew he could not do it. For years he had forthrightly exposed the radical modernism of many of the church's leaders and called for biblical separation from them, He could not now conscientiously repudiate that stand even though imprisonment and possible death should be in store. He politely but firmly stated he could not join the union.

As he anticipated, hc was eventually called down to the headquarters of the secret police whose building was near the Dutch Embassy. The Christian chancellor of that time, Chancellor Kok, described to the writer on one occasion the terrible sounds of torture he often heard coming from that building. Pastor Wang was prepared for the worst and went dressed in warm clothes for winter imprisonment, although it was still sometime before winter. After lengthy interrogation, which lasted all day, however, he was released with stern warnings of the need to comply.

He went on with his work, ignoring the warning, and later was once again called down. This time he was sure it was the end, but again he was delivered, and continued his faithful ministry throughout the war, later writing a book on his experiences.[16] Ten years after those experiences he was again to be under arrest, by an even more ruthless power, that of Communism. The grounds of his arrest were the same as before: refusal to unite with those whom he knew to be deniers of the faith, the false leaders of the puppet church. With great courage and faithfulness he exposed them for what they were and warned the church. Like Daniel of old, he discharged his responsibility and trustingly left the results in the hands of the Lord of the Lion's Den.

---

1. Miss Elisabeth Whewell, missionary of the Mino Mission, working at that time in Ogaki, Gifu Ken.

2. Miss Elizabeth Whewell, writing in *The Sunday School Times*, March 1, 1941.

3. Frank Gibney, *Five Gentlemen of Japan*, p. 204. Charles E. Tuttle Co., Tokyo, 1954.

4. *S.S. Times, op. cit.*

5. Phyllis Argall, *My Life with the Enemy*. Note p. 98 ff.

6. Rev. Bruce Hunt, lecturing on "The Pre-War Church-Shrine Struggle in Korea," in Karui zawa, Japan, 1953.

7. When the Presbyterian (USA) Board of Foreign Missions ordered its Korea Mission to turn its schools over to the Korean Presbyterian Church presbyteries, and thus free them to go to the Shinto shrines to bow, Dr. J.G. Holdcroft, former

chairman of the mission's executive committee (1926-'28 and 1933-'36), resigned from the board and church in protest and joined the Independent Board for Presbyterian Foreign Missions in 1940. Dr. and Mrs. William Chisholm and Miss M. Hanson did likewise.

8. A. Ebisawa, *Contemporary Japan, op, cit.*

9. J.G. Vos, "A Review of the Foreign Missions Conference of North America's Fiftieth Annual Report," pp. 17-8. The Evangelical Fellowship Inc., Pittsburgh, 1944.

10. Bruce Hunt, *op. cit.*

11. Baker, *op. cit.*, pp. 188-9.

12. Bertha S. Byram, M.D., *Brought Before Governors for a Testimony,* p. 12. The Independent Board for Presbyterian Foreign Missions, Philadelphia, 1943.

13. *Ibid.*, p. 13.

14. Vos, *A Review, op. cit.*, pp. 30-1.

15. *Ibid.*, p. 13.

16. Wang Ming-Tao, *Deliverance from the Tiger's Den*, Peiping, China, 1946.

6

The Record of the United Church in Japan

"The path of compromise for the churches of the empire led ever downwards until they were almost the complete slaves of the pagan state."

The year 1940 in Japan saw a tremendous impetus towards the church union movement. For fifteen years previously, committees had met occasionally to discuss the possibility of some sort of organic integration among churches, with no real progress. April 1940, however, saw the government promulgation of the "Religious Bodies Law," elsewhere in the empire, as has been noted, called "The Law to Control the Religious Institution and Propagator." This law was the real father of the *Nihon Kirisuto Kyodan*, the United Church of Christ in Japan. Even its wartime head, Mitsuru Tomita, seemed to admit this in his report to the executive committee in December 1945. "As the United Church was built upon this law, it is, I hope, fitting to take up this subject for your deliberation," he reported.[1] The extent to which the Kyodan was "built upon" this law has been pointed out. "The constitution of the United Church parallels the Religious Bodies Law of 1940 and is completely harmonious with it. That law stipulates at every essential point that the church or religious body can do nothing without 'approval of the competent minister.' The minister in every case was the government's Minister of Education."[2]

The story of Christianity in Japan during the war is largely the story of the Kyodan and its activities under the Religious Bodies Law. It is a sad story, but one that needs to be put down on the record that all might know why evangelicals cannot work within its organization, and why most of them separated from it in the postwar years. The story does have a few brighter spots, however, of men who, even though they were in the compromised position of being enmeshed in the Kyodan, and under the iniquitous control law, yet gave their testimony that Jehovah was greater than the mythical sun goddess or the emperor, and suffered in jail for it, some even to death. The brightest witness of all, however, came from those who stayed out of the entangling alliance of the United Church and bore their testimony for their sovereign Lord, against all compromise with Shinto ideology, right through long imprisonment to the brink of death. The Kyodan's record through the war years needs to be examined and followed with the story of some who gave a different witness.

Kyodan Formed Under Government Coercion

The government indicated that under the Religious Bodies Law, the text of which was released in 1939, recognition and tax exemption would be given to those religious bodies receiving government licenses after registration, but that only larger bodies could hope to be successful in obtaining them. No specific size was stated but upon inquiry the minister gave his private ruling that a religious body should have at least 50 churches and 5,000 members. Of this Baker writes, "Nothing more sweeping in its effect on the life of the Christian church in Japan in modern times ever took place than this unofficial private ruling of the Ministry of Education. For in this ruling the United Church of Christ in Japan was born."[3] It might be well to note here that these quotations come from one who, as an American ecumenicist, shows a marked disinclination to be critical of the Kyodan, but who nonetheless is compelled to recognize the facts just quoted. This numbers qualification made many churches that, up to this time, had no interest in church union suddenly prize it very highly. The ministry's urgent advice to the churches to unite was an added incentive.

On October 17, 1940, a mass meeting was held to approve the formation of a united Protestant Church and in June, 1941, thirty-two church groups came together to form eleven blocs in a federated union. These group or bloc systems were as follows: 1) Presbyterian (*Nikki*); 2) Methodist, Methodist Protestant and Holy-Garden (*Seian*); 3) Congregational, Brethren, Evangelical, Disciples and Friends; 4) Baptist; 5) Evangelical Lutheran; 6) Holiness (*Sei*); 7) Pentecostal, Jesus (Restoration), Holiness (*Seiketsu*); 8) Free Methodist, Nazarene, Alliance (*Domei*), World Mission; 9) Kiyome (Holiness), Free Church; 10) Independent; and 11) Salvation Army. The Episcopal Church at first did not join but in 1943 split on the issue with sixty churches coming into the union as individual churches. The moderator was appointed the Kyodan's official representative to Ise to report its founding to the sun goddess. In November 1941, the Kyodan received its government license and recognition, although the blocs were reduced to seven. Only a few smaller groups and individual churches stayed out and were not recognized as religious bodies but as religious associations. As such they were put under the supervision of the local police, rather than under the Ministry of Education. One year later, November 1942, the government exercised its prerogative under the Religious Bodies Law and ordered the Kyodan to disband its blocs and amalgamate into a real, united church.

Professor Yanagita, in his excellent little history, has commented, "In November of the next year, at the second general assembly, the bloc system was abolished, although the promise of its continuance had been one of the main points effecting the unification. This general meeting also decided to make a patriotic contribution toward the purchase of war planes."[4]

How was it, however, that all these churches, the great majority, could so readily put themselves under the controlling measures of the Religious Bodies Law? Baker describes the purpose of the law in these words: "In all matters touching organization of the churches, the state's desire was to streamline all democracy out of the organization and delegate responsibility to one church and one *torisha* (superintendent) only, which could be easily controlled and through a vertical line of authority hand down the state's commands. This was the sum purpose of the Religious Bodies Law of 1940." Later he adds, "In short, they wanted the church in a position where they could control it. This was the reason the Protestants were coerced into union in 1940 and 1941."[5]

The independent testimonies of two Japanese pastors who were present at the organization of the Kyodan, and saw the pressure of the government upon the groups to coerce them into union, are very interesting. Pastor Tokiwa of Tokyo's

Grace Reformed Church has written, "The government thought of uniting to-gether all Protestants in Japan and of ruling them. For this reason, oppression was inflicted upon the churches. I don't think it would have been possible to organize the Kyodan without such pressure. Such being the case, the Kyodan was organized by the official, unwritten pressure and by the efforts of those people who persisted in the union of the churches…. The worst thing before God was at this [organiza-tion] ceremony they bowed low with respect toward the Imperial Palace (*Kyujo yohai*), which is idolatry and a deadly sin against God."[6]

One who was active in the innermost circles during the organization of the Kyodan has also written a very revealing account of the government's goal and compulsion in forming this United Church. The Rev. Shigetoshi Taniguchi, pastor of Kami no Kyokai (Church) of Tamagawa, Tokyo, and president of the Tamagawa Sei Gakuin (School), has written:

> I participated in the formation of the Kyodan as a delegate of the Independent Church bloc, and knew what took place. In addition, I was well acquainted with the Chief of the Religious Bureau of the Education Ministry, Mr. Nakajima, who succeeded Mr. Matsuo. He was one of my school mates in the Third High School, my junior by one class. I often talked with him and became quite aware of what was taking place, including the facts I give here. Further, on several occasions I was asked by the Army Paymaster, Lt. General Nobusuke Hibiki who was a member of the Fujimicho church, to negotiate with him. The General used his influence to aid in the formation of the N.K. Kyodan.
>
> After the Sino-Japanese incident began, the military authorities were very anxious to control the thinking of the people throughout the nation. These au-thorities achieved their long-cherished aim by appointing General Sadao Araki (ex-War Minister) to the post of Minister of Education, which post he kept through 1938–'39 during the cabinets of both Hiranuma and Konoe. General Araki successfully pushed the Religious Bodies Bill through the Imperial Diet in 1939 and it became law.
>
> At that time the Government authorities obviously entertained the goal of forming a Religious Association into which the three main religions of Shinto-ism, Buddhism and Christianity would be integrated. This association was to be a strongly regimented one, strictly conformed to the ideology of the military, its purpose being to make the religions more efficiently serve the war effort. Only

these three religions were to be officially recognized. Further, the plan included a program for uniting all the Protestant and Roman Catholic churches. The Greek Orthodox Church was not to be given recognition.

Eventually Christian delegates of various denominations met together to discuss the unification of their churches. Finally, at a great national Christian Convention, held at Aoyama University on October 17th, 1940, and attended by the properly appointed delegates of all denominations, they proclaimed their resolution to unify all their churches into one organization. The General Conference for the formation of the United Church of Christ in Japan (Kyodan) was held the next year on June 24th and 25th, 1941, at the Fujimicho Church. It was there decided that the Apostles Creed would be sufficient basis for the union.

The constitution of the new United Church was almost ready to be adopted by the delegates when, because of the determined objections of the Nihon Kirisuto Kyokai (Kyu Niki) to it, the Methodists and Congregationalists insisted that they proceed even if it meant the omission of the N.K.K. The Chairman of the day, Mr. Yoshimune Abe, together with Mr. Mitsuru Tomida (elected Superintendent), keeping the convention adjourned for a while and its members awaiting their announcement, hastened over to the Education Ministry to inquire further about the Government's plan for Christianity. When they returned they brought word of the authorities' firm determination to outlaw any denomination or individual church rejecting the union. Thereupon those opposing the union surrendered and approved the group system (by which all churches joined one of eleven groups which in turn united together to form the Kyodan).

To sum up, it was the Army's objective, through their spokesman General Araki who was made Minister of Education, to compel the churches to unite in order both to keep them in line with the military's Shintoist ideology and to make them more efficiently serve the war effort. In 1944 the United Church joined the wartime Patriotic Religious Association as the third member, along with the Buddhists and Shintoists, thereby bringing the Army's plan for a united Religious Association to completion.[7]

The government's intention and compulsion were obvious.

Kyodan's Doctrine Controlled by Religious Bodies Law

In addition to giving the government minister absolute veto powers, and control over the church's operation and doctrine, the Religious Bodies Law contained such statements as this of Article 26: "In case a teacher or missionary has contravened the restriction, prohibition or suspension of work provided for in Article 16 (i.e., forbidding teaching which 'disturbs peace or order, or proves contrary to the duties of national subjects,' or if he 'commits an act prejudicial to public interest') ... he shall be punished with penal servitude or imprisonment."[8] J.G. Vos, commenting on this, wrote: "It must be realized that the Government regards participation in the rites of State Shinto (including *yohai* and *jinja sampai*) as 'the duty of national subjects.' A religious body which opposes this may have its license cancelled, and a religious teacher who does so may be suspended from office in a religious body by action of the civil magistrates."[9] He states categorically, "This is an iniquitous totalitarian law.... It makes the State supreme in the sphere of religion and reduces the Church to servile bondage to the totalitarian authorities."[10]

Baker points out how the government, through this law, actually did control the doctrine of the Kyodan. He says,

> By far the most flagrant case of the Christian church's yielding its prerogatives to the state was the dictation which the churches accepted concerning their polity and creed.... The ministry did assert its authority over two prominent items in the Christian creed. One was the belief in God as creator of the world. The other was the belief in a final divine judgment of all history. These beliefs "endangered" the state in that they challenged the Shinto story.... When I asked a member of the United Church why it had never written a creed, he replied, "The *Mombusho* (Ministry of Education) kept objecting to certain passages as being alien to Japanese thought." ... The wording of the (Kyodan) catechism is a sample of the way the church juggled words and compromised with the government, satisfying themselves with a brief statement of thoroughly orthodox belief, and at the same time satisfying the government by not using the more direct words of the Apostles Creed, "Maker of heaven and earth," and "From whence he shall come to judge the quick and the dead."[11]

The long years of indoctrination in the Shinto ideology, from kindergarten to profession, plus the life of accommodation to and compromise with it, coupled with the stimulus of the war psychology and fear of offending public opinion, had left the church in general, and its leadership in particular, weak and impotent, unable and unwilling to stand up for the sovereign rights of the Lord she professed against the demands of the pagan state.

The tragic downward course of the Kyodan during the war years is summed up in one paragraph in the report of the Supreme Commander for the Allied Powers on Japan's religions. "Persecution of certain denominations occurred. The Holiness Church, which finally joined the Church of Christ, and the Seventh Day Adventist Church which did not, were ordered dissolved. The Salvation Army was ordered to revise its military terminology. The spy mania, abolishment of Sunday as a holiday, the evacuation of women and children from large cities, and the mobilization of pastors to munitions factories all caused a drop in church and Sunday School attendance. Services, however were continued throughout the war, and the practices of bowing toward the

Women being trained for a last-ditch stand after the fall of Saipan, September 1944

imperial palace and praying for the soldiers who had died, and for those at the front, were gradually added to the services. In 1944, the Church of Christ in Japan, along with the Roman Catholic Church, joined the Japan Wartime Patriotic Religious Association, in cooperation with the Shinto and Buddhist bodies."[12]

Thus the churches, which for many decades had flirted with the Shinto ideology by allowing their children to be trained in it through the educational system, and had cooperated with the demands for control by the Shinto-militarists, at last found themselves actually welded to the Shinto enemy of Christ and participating in its heathen worship.

The downward path continued throughout the war with the church seeming to trim its sails to go with the winds of the *kamikaze* from whatever directions they blew. Baker's description of it is worth quoting.

When a religion accommodates itself completely to the social milieu in which it moves, it becomes chameleon-like and indistinguishable from the environment which surrounds it. This was the way in which Christianity in wartime Japan sacrificed its message and lost its uniqueness and evangelizing power. The sharpest criticisms I heard of Christianity in Japan did not come from foreigners but from sensitive Japanese themselves, who said that wartime Christianity failed in Japan because it offered the people nothing more than they could get from the government's propaganda.[13]

Part of the Kyodan's Wartime Record

That this was true can be seen by examining the record of some of the Kyodan's wartime activities. "In so far as the activities and utterances of the leaders of the Christian movement in Japan are open for objective examination," wrote Holtom, "they show a purpose to fit Christianity fully into the scheme of comprehensive regimentation demanded by the state."[14] Some illustrations will verify this. Baker points out that "[o]n numerous occasions the United Church of Christ in Japan (Kyodan) was guilty of handing down governmental orders to its local churches. One of these cases had to do with the officially prescribed five-minute ceremony of bowing to the Emperor and praying for the war heroes just preceding every Christian service of worship. It was a compulsory ritual, and if for any reason it was ever neglected the pastor was immediately taken by the police for questioning."[15] This Shinto encroachment on Christian worship, and desecration of the house of God, was practiced by the licensed churches throughout Japan. One pastor of a large city church, shortly after the war, apologetically told the writer, in defense of his actions, that he had held this five-minute *Yohai* service five minutes before his Sunday morning worship service began, and thus it was not so bad. The fact the most consecrated Christians deliberately came late to avoid this distant worship of the emperor testifies as to how they really felt about it.

The Kyodan also carried out the government's directive to revise the hymn book so as to conform to the Shinto nationalism. Of this "special wartime hymnal," Baker wrote that it was "an expurgated collection of hymns which clearly showed the church's willingness to yield to the state on a vital matter of Christian practice."[16] He cites as one illustration the removal from all hymns of the regal word *o-kimi* as referring to Jesus Christ since the same word is used to designate the emperor as sovereign royalty. All reference to Christ as "King of kings" was abolished since such was abhorrent to the Shinto-militarists. Such hymns as "Onward, Christian Soldiers" and "A Mighty Fortress Is Our God" were dropped. Still worse, hymns specially written expressing the Shinto expansionist ideology in terms of the Christian missionary program were put into the new hymnal.

A Presbyterian missionary of liberal persuasion has since given the following descriptions of the attitudes and actions of the Kyodan's members during the war. "The united Church of Christ in Japan, called the Nippon Kirisuto Kyodan, that had been consummated under governmental pressure in 1941, achieved complete centralization.... The church was faced with a dilemma—nay, more than one and it found it hard to accept one horn to the absolute exclusion of the other. In baldest terms it was a choice between Japan and the West, between Caesar and God, between myth and fact, between totalitarianism and individualism.... They believed that it was better to make some compromise with Caesar than to have a head-on collision with the militarists.... Those responsible for the welfare of the church also felt that it was better to stay on the job and compromise than to go into hiding in order to avoid the choice between Caesar and God."[17]

In addition, the Kyodan officials, at the insistence of the government, tried to prescribe the sermon topics for all its pastors for a whole year, as prescription of the topics was required also at Shinto and Buddhist services. In their literature throughout the war, they minimized the fact that Christmas celebrated the birth of Christ and emphasized rather that it was the anniversary of the death of the late Emperor Taisho. They made no effort to try to protect their pastors from conscription but rather actively cooperated in the conscription of some into hard labor. A few years after the war the writer was talking to a group of orthodox pastors who had withdrawn from the Kyodan immediately after the war. In speaking of that church's wartime activities one of them said, "When the Kyodan was asked to demonstrate its patriotism by asking for volunteers to work in the coal mines, whose names were sent into the government as volunteers without their consent?" And then pointing to the group he added, "Ours! We were known to be orthodox and in opposition to their betrayals of Christ." Some of these men,[18] who were active pastors and had no experience with hard manual work since their youth, were put into the coal mines and were required to do backbreaking work that nearly killed them, a number coming down with consumption because of it.

The Kyodan's wartime literature was close to, if not inspired by, the official government propaganda line. The *Sunday School Teacher's Magazine* was one of the publications of the Board of Sunday Schools, of which the first new postwar head of the Kyodan, Michio Kozakai, was bureau chief. In it frequently such articles as the one entitled "Obey the Imperial Rescript" would appear. One of the sentences in that read, "If we obey the imperial rescript and do our service to the Emperor, we are at the same time obeying and serving our God."[19] Almost the whole article is taken up with the importance of serving the emperor, with a brief concluding word on the necessity also of serving Christ, in spite of the fact that the basis of imperial rescripts was always the polytheistic ideology of the divine imperative stemming from the emperor's connection with the divine ancestress.

"Christian" Propagators of Shinto Ideology

The tragic extent to which the church had accommodated itself to the polytheistic state during this period can be seen not only in the actions of the Kyodan but also in those of some of its individual leaders. One of those who strove most diligently, and wrote most prolifically, to bridge the gulf between Christianity and Shinto ideology was the General Secretary of the NCC of Japan, Mr. Arika Ebisawa, who continued in that office until 1955. Three of his well-known articles were, "The Relation Between the Ethics of Bushido and Christianity" (*Bushido* being the code of the warrior which is deeply rooted in the principle of vengeance); "New Apologetics for the New Age" (a defense of the military expansion on the Asiatic continent); and "Christianity and the Establishment of the New Order in East Asia," from which last article the following is a quotation.

> What then is the plan for the long-term reconstruction of East Asia? Its purpose is that of realizing the vision emblazoned on the banner, "The world one family" (*hakko ichiu*); and that purpose, we must recognize afresh, coincides spontaneously with the fundamental faith of Christianity.... This is the Christian conception of the Kingdom of God. The basis of the Japanese spirit also consists in this; and thus, wonderful to relate, it is one with Christianity. Nay, this must indeed be the Great Way of Heaven and Earth.[20]

Early in 1940, the NCC published a series of four propaganda pamphlets. One of these was entitled "Patriotism of the Spirit and Christianity" and was written by Mr. Saburo Imai, a Methodist pastor and former chaplain of Methodist Aoyama Gakuin middle school. The following quotation illustrates the method of accommodation undertaken by the writer. "It is our mission to protect the Chinese people from having their whole body cast into Gehenna, even though their right eye must be plucked out. With love in our hearts we have resolved on the completion of the Holy War."[21] In summarizing the accommodation of that period, Holtom writes, "Christians in high official positions have performed obeisance before the altars of the spirits of the

Grief before Yasukuni Shrine as apologies are offered to the spirits of the war dead for the defeat, August 15, 1945

Meiji Emperor and his consort at the Meiji Jingu (Shrine) of Tokyo and before the spirits of the war dead at Yasukuni Shrine on Kudan Hill; outstanding Christian leaders have announced Christian programs before the spirit of the sun goddess at the Grand Imperial Shrine at Ise; and Christian schools within Japan proper have participated almost without exception in attendance at shrine ceremonies."[22] One noteworthy exception to the latter was the Kobe Theological Seminary, which preferred to be closed in 1941 by official order rather than compromise on this point.

In 1938, the writer heard an illustration of a rather fantastic effort to accommodate Christian doctrine to Shinto Nationalist ideology. An official in Osaka, desiring to determine the position of churches of that area concerning the relation of the Christian God to the authority of the emperor, sent out a questionnaire to them with a series of questions covering this subject. A group of Congregational pastors, with a novel apologetic, replied that they considered that the Godhead consisted of four persons: the Father, the Son, the Holy Spirit and the Japanese emperor. Further, they taught that the God of Christianity has a twofold incarnation, the savior of the soul, Jesus Christ, and the political savior of the world, the Japanese emperor. When these replies were turned in, the responsible individuals were immediately called down to the police headquarters and severely reprimanded for blaspheming the name of the emperor by putting him on a level with the

Christian God rather than holding that he was the supreme being of the universe. It was reported that at least one of these pastors was imprisoned for this offense.

One of the most dismal records of all was that of the many Christian leaders who made periodic pilgrimages to the sun goddess shrine at Ise to present *norito*, or prayers. One of these prayers was presented in I. Okino's *Jinja Mondai* and read in part: "Bring it to pass that the subjects of the empire may quicken and elevate the Japanese spirit as in the Age of the Gods; that they may exalt the glory of the national life; that they may make the power of the Empire to shine ever higher, ever wider, and for eternity; and grant that Japan may become the model for all nations.... Bring it to pass that all things may be done according to the Way of the Gods.... This we ask in solemn awe."[23] That those who were recognized as Christian leaders could perform such acts of idolatry without being repudiated by their churches for it, is further evidence of the extent to which the thinking of the churches had become conditioned to compromise by the early 1940s.

One of those who went to this shrine to pray was Dr. Toyohiko Kagawa who, as has been noted already, also consented to make a tour of the churches in Korea and Manchukuo to help persuade them to carry out the government's directives concerning shrine worship. While recognizing Kagawa's contributions in social welfare work, it is true that his complete compromise on the shrine problem, together with his liberal theology, has made his ministry in Japan a great handicap to the development of true Christianity. A sample of his liberalism is seen in the following quotation from one of his books. "We do not know in what form the resurrection did come. Whether it was in the flesh as the Gospels teach or in the spiritual body as Paul tells us, it makes no difference. Anyway Jesus was truly raised in the hearts of his disciples. Here is the beginning of Christianity. If you want to take it as a superstition you may take it so."[24]

In a more recent utterance, Kagawa has written the following concerning John 6:53: "As a social engineer, this saying of Jesus becomes a guide for my daily program: 'Unless you drink of my blood and eat my flesh you will have no life in you.' This means that I (and my nation) must give our very lives to heal the world's crimes. Unless some nation is ready to take the risk, to pay the debt of sin and crime, crime will not be redeemed. This is the deepest principle of Christian theology, as it is the deepest truth of life itself."[25]

An evangelism based on this kind of an understanding of the meaning of Christ's resurrection and atonement could not result in souls redeemed from the superstitious polytheism of Shintoism nor hearts filled with the desire to serve Christ with undivided love and loyalty. It was this kind of preaching which, failing to convince the people of the uniqueness of Christ and His claim for the total allegiance of men, left them in the time of threatened persecution saying, as one did to Baker, "It was wise for every Japanese family to have a *kamidana* in one's home in case the police come to examine us for our patriotic loyalty."[26]

The Ideology of the 2600th Anniversary

One of the greatest united acts of mass idolatry participated in by the Christians of that period was committed by those who assembled to make the decision to organize the Kyodan. The mass meeting assembled at Aoyama Gakuin on

Celebrating the 2600th anniversary of the empire, 1940, in Meiji Shrine's Outer Grounds

October 17, 1940, in celebration of the mythical founding of the empire by the descendant of the sun goddess, and decided to "complete the union of all the Christian churches ... revive the spirit (Shinto terminology), elevate morals and renew lives." The meeting began by worshiping the Imperial Palace from a distance (*Kyujo yohai*). A specially composed hymn was sung, glorifying the emperor and connecting him with the mythological divine ancestress. Delegates then went in a body to Meiji Shrine to do obeisance, a fact which may seem incredible to evangelicals today but which is nonetheless true. Those

Representatives of the government, civic organizations, the Christian church, and a platoon of soliders journey to Meiji Shrine to worship on the 2600th anniversary, 1940

who did have a conscience on the matter tried to reassure themselves with the statements of both the government and the NCC that these places of Shinto polytheistic worship, being state shrines, were not "religious" (*shukyo*) places. Thus did the Christian church render unto Casear the things which belonged to God alone.

Ruin of emperor's palace after fire bombing

The writer has been assured, however, by a missionary who claims to have authoritative information on the matter, that the Presbyterian (*Nikki*) representatives present did not make the pilgrimage to the shrine, although those of other evangelical bodies such as the Holiness groups did. He has written, "The Nihon Kirisuto Kyokai (not Kyodan) refused to send delegations to Shinto shrines, refrained from engaging in *Kyujo Yohai* at its meetings, and also refused to set up *Taima* (symbol of Ise Jingu) in the churches."[27] Another group of Christians, led by pastors, that year received permission to hold a parade from downtown to the Imperial Palace plaza, to the traditional spot in front of the double bridge, where they did *yohai* obeisance, at midnight.

Evidence that *yohai* involved more than a bow to the emperor as a human sovereign lay all around. All allegiance to him was declared to be on the basis that he was the divine descendant of the sun goddess. That very year, in the Diet, the statement was made that *yohai* was offered to the sun goddess through the emperor and her local palace shrine, the *Kashikodokoro*, at which he alone officiated. Each year on October 17, the Feast of *Kannamesai* (First Fruits), the emperor himself did *yohai* towards the sun goddess's Grand Shrine at Ise. Surely this was clear evidence that *yohai* involved much more than recognition of a human sovereign, and that inextricably attached to it was sun goddess worship, the word itself meaning "distant worship."

The Kyodan was organized into fourteen ecclesiastical districts, five of which were outside Japan proper. One of these was the Manchu Missionary District. In the spring of 1942, when all the "Mission" churches there were welded into one

United Church, special celebrations were held in the various areas. A missionary of the Reformed Presbyterian Mission in Manchukuo has written a very interesting account of the "Dedication of the United Church in Manchukuo." Her description of the program committee's plight is revealing. "The first number, by imperial command, was the reading of the Rescript, followed by the performance of the Shinto rites. After these were duly recorded, it was proposed that devotional exercises follow after the manner of Christian churches. They tried to choose a hymn, but none seemed suitable to sing just after worshipping the Shinto deities, so they decided to omit the singing. Then they had the same difficulty in choosing a selection from the Bible. So it seemed best to have only a prayer, but no one of the group was willing to make the prayer. Worshipping two different gods at the same meeting was likely to produce complications!"[28]

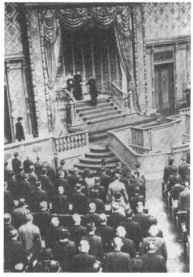

The emperor hands down a Rescript in the Diet, December 28, 1946

She then goes on to tell how finally one man made a suggestion.

"I perceive that in this matter we must wholly depart from God. I suggest that we simply omit all of this and be rid of the dilemma." But another declared, "We can't do such a thing! We can't leave God out! Isn't this a union of Christian churches?" So eventually another agreed to write a special hymn for the occasion and the prayer also. She concludes, "So this sin of omission was avoided, but no mention was made of the sin of worshipping another god in the face of Him who said, 'Thou shalt have no other gods before me.'"[29] This sin, the great sin of putting the commands and fear of men, and their mythical gods, above faithfulness to the living and true God, was the ever-present sin in the church union movement which brought the Kyodan into existence.

The path of compromise for the churches of the empire led ever downwards until they were almost the complete slaves of the pagan state. No objective appraisal could avoid this conclusion. The U.S. Army's unbiased summation of the events of this period will bear this out, and with the following quotations we will bring to a conclusion this sad chapter in the church's history.

Great pressure was exerted on Buddhist, Shinto and Christian sects to unite and, in certain cases, to eliminate parts of their scriptures and teachings.... In the early decades of the modern era, Christians remained aloof from shrine worship, but, in 1940, they participated fully, even to the extent of sending representatives to report at Ise Shrine regarding ecclesiastical activities.... Only a few Christian groups refused to participate in such worship. The others permitted themselves to drift with the nationalistic current flowing so strongly through Japanese life.... Religious bodies had been sufficiently disciplined by then (wartime) so that there was no question about their cooperating. What the world was not prepared for was their almost complete submission to the state in matters of theology and worship as well as in patriotic service. For, during the years from 1941 to 1945, religion was almost the completely subservient handmaiden of the state.[30]

---

1. Baker, *op, cit.,* p. 41.

2. *Ibid.,* p. 34.

3. *Ibid.,* p. 40.

4. Yanagita, *op. cit.,* p. 70.

5. Baker, *op. cit.,* pp 42, 79.

6. T. Tokiwa, "Kyodan Formed Without Pressure?," *Japan Harvest,* Vol. 5, No. 2. 1957, Spring, p. 23.

7. Shigetoshi Taniguchi, "The Real Circumstances Surrounding the Establishment of the Nihon Kirisuto Kyodan," *The Bible Times,* Vol. VII, No. 2, 1957, p. 23. Translated by Hideyo Nagase and the author.

8. Religious Bodies Law, official English translation, as received by the author in 1939.

9. Vos, *Christian Mission, op. cit.,* p. 13.

10. Vos, *A Review, op. cit.,* p. 18.

11. Baker, *op. cit.,* pp. 34, 38-9.

12. Bunce, *op. cit.,* p. 155.

13. Baker, *op. cit.,* p. 69.

14. Holtom, *op. cit.,* p. 101.

15. Baker, *op. cit.,* p. 31.

16. *Ibid.,* p. 31.

17. William C. Kerr, *Japan Begins Again,* pp. 84, 88-9. Friendship Press, New

York, 1949.

18. Pastors of the former Nikki Church who, in October 1945, withdrew from the Kyodan and organized the Reformed Church in Japan, based on the Westminster Standards.

19. Baker, *op. cit.*, p. 26.

20. Holtom, *op. cit.*, p. 109-10.

21. *Ibid.*, p. 109.

22. *Ibid.*, p. 100.

23. Holtom, *op. cit.*, p. 100-1.

24. Kagawa, *The Religion of Jesus,* p. 103.

25. T. Kagawa, *Japan Christian Quarterly*, October 1955, p. 312.

26. Baker, *op. cit.*, p. 70.

27. G.K. Chapman, in a letter dated February 18, 1953.

28. Miss Rose Huston, quoted in Vos, *A Review, op. cit.,* p. 28.

29. *Ibid.*, p. 28-9.

30. Bunce, *op. cit.*, pp. 36-9.

7

The Witness of Some Who Were Persecuted

"The brightest testimony of all to the effect that the Lord Christ was the only Savior, and supreme sovereign over the universe, came from men who could make it consistently because they refused to enter the Kyodan or put themselves under the evil Religious Bodies Law."

The Hokkaido Nikki Pastors

Even within the Kyodan, however, there were some pastors who, although they had submitted to the compromise of Kyodan membership and that of registration under the evil Religious Bodies Law, would not further yield their witness to the Kingship of Christ. In Sapporo, Hokkaido, Rinzo Onomura was pastor of a large Nihon Kirisuto Kyokai church and chairman of the board of directors of the Hokusei Gakuin girls' school. This school had not sought government recognition and up to 1941 had not been asked to send their students out to the shrine nor read the Rescript on Education nor bow to the emperor's portrait. That year, however, officials came to the school and informed them that these ceremonies must be performed. Onomura replied that this could not be done and that they would close the school before yielding on this point. He was called in to the police headquarters for lengthy questioning at which time he admitted having opposed going out to the local Maruyama shrine. He also denied belief in the divinity of the emperor and the historicity of the sun goddess. Further, he readily admitted that early in 1942 he had declared from his pulpit that Christians all over the world were still brothers. Such opinions were considered to be darkest blasphemy. The school was closed and Onomura was held in prison for eight months pending a trial.

One of the darkest records of the Kyodan was that during this time its Hokkaido District head, Kyokusho Manno (a Methodist), tried to take Onomura's church away from him and give it to another. Manno himself had placed a *kamidana* in his own front room. During the three-month trial some of the non-Christian Hokkaido University professors came to testify for Onomura and he was eventually given his release. Others of the former Nikki pastors and elders in Hokkaido, including pastors Miyoshi, K. Yamashita, and Sasaki, and elders Takiuchi and Dr. Togasaki, were also arrested and imprisoned for various lengths of time, on similar charges to those laid against Onomura. One of the deep grievances many of the Nikki pastors had against the Kyodan, from which a large group separated in 1951, was that after the war there was no act of apology nor repentance on the part of the Kyodan for its Kyokusho's dismal rejection of these men who would not deny that Jehovah was greater than Amaterasu.

The Holiness Pastors

The largest group in the Kyodan to have police charges brought against it was the *Seiyokai,* the Holiness Church. Early in the morning of July 26, 1942, the police called on the homes of forty-six of their pastors and arrested them. Mr. Akiji Kurumada, the group's head, and Toyozo Abe, its general affairs chairman, were two of these. The arrest, undertaken not by the Education Ministry, which had jurisdiction over church affairs, but by the Ministry of Home Affairs, which controlled the civil police, came as a complete surprise to these men. Abe, some years later, reported, "I was a devoted Christian, all that I considered a model citizen, and a loyal, patriotic Japanese. I could think of no reason that the police should want me. I make this element of surprise so clear to you, because there was nothing in our behavior as a church which was intended to provoke the political powers that be."[1]

There was much in the behavior of anyone who opposed shrine obeisance or *yohai* to provoke the officials, but that was not the issue on which the Holiness Church pastors stood, as has already been noted. The charges brought against them now were not of such a nature. They concerned their preaching that Jesus Christ would return to earth and that then every knee must bow before Him. This teaching was held to be objectionable since it meant that the emperor too would have to bow and that Christ's kingship was superior to his.

After much questioning, Abe was given a document to sign which contained a slanted report of his answers that was very incriminating. He refused to sign it, was beaten and imprisoned for 288 days, in which time he saw the sunlight for only twenty minutes. The officials finally agreed to rewrite his confession, but although a few of the most glaring incriminations were removed he felt he still could not sign. After a month of argument he decided to sign in order to bring his case to trial. Before the procurator, however, Abe repudiated his signed confession on the grounds that it had been coerced. He was given a hearing before a grand jury in February 1944, and was finally allowed to answer certain written questions freely. On the basis of these, new charges were prepared against him and signed by him.

He was brought to trial on July 3, 1944, on the evidence of the signed statements, together with twelve other leading Holiness pastors. Their defense was that their beliefs were religious and lacking in political implications, and that they were faithful to the secular power. On December 27, 1944, however, Abe and five others were given three years imprisonment and five years probation, the heaviest sentence, and the rest various sentences, but none less than a year. They were not released until October 11, 1945, when MacArthur's directive granting freedom to all "thought" prisoners was issued. All the Holiness pastors had been called in for questioning during those years, some fifty-seven undergoing long prison terms. Two died in prison and two others shortly after their release, while a number of others had their health ruined at the hands of the police and their jailers.[2]

Some Who Withstood All Accommodation

The brightest testimony of all to the effect that the Lord Christ was the only Savior and supreme sovereign over the universe came from men who could make it consistently because they refused to enter the Kyodan or put themselves under the evil Religious Bodies Law. Two such were independent brethren, Kitamoto and Fujimoto. They were arrested in August 1941 for their uncompromising witness to the supremacy of Jehovah over all others whom men called gods, and their insistence that Christians could not bow before any other deity than the risen and returning Lord. Their preaching that Christ would return to earth someday, when all men must bow before Him, was especially detested. One was given a three-year sentence and the other a four-year sentence, but both were warned that unless they changed their views they would not even be released on the expiration of these sentences. Both were still in prison when the American forces arrived more than four years later. Pastor Kikuchi of the Mino Mission was also incarcerated but was later released in order to provide for his large family. Still another independent brother who was arrested was Tamezo Yamanaka, who had been a very active and fearless evangelist. He was picked up on March 26, 1942, and taken to an Osaka procurator's office. Like the others he was tried under "the law for the maintenance of the public peace," the charge being that he was "assumed to be in suspicion of crime for teaching the following: ... Jesus Christ in establishing the said millennium will destroy and sweep away all nations on the earth, and consequently he (the accused) insists that our Tenno Sovereignty shall also be abolished. At the same time he gives his arbitrary decision that there is no God other than this God of the Trinity. Furthermore, he insists that our Amaterasu Omikami of Ise Shrine is nothing but an idol. The accused engaged in propagating the said teaching and denied our national polity (*kokutai*). He organized and directed the group with the purpose of propagating the matters which debase the dignity of our shrine and our respectful Imperial House."[3]

As one reads these excerpts from the official charges, he almost feels transported back into the nineteenth chapter of Acts and the accusations made against the apostles there. Had it been the practice of Christians throughout Japan during the previous decades to give such testimony against Ise and the foolishness of the whole Shinto ideology, backing it up with such steadfast refusal to have any part in any of its ceremonies, in the schools or elsewhere, the tragic event of the Pacific War might well have been avoided. Yamanaka was given a three-year sentence and informed there would be no release until he changed his opinions. In prison, existing on unsanitarily prepared food and suffering from malnutrition, he came to the very brink of death, doctors even declaring, one cold, wintry day that the end had come and that he could not survive until evening. He was placed on a rough straw mat for death—but the Lord had other plans. He revived, although he was not released until the day the emperor announced the surrender of the nation on the radio, August 15, 1945. That day showed his jailers clearly his forthright assertion that the sun goddess was a mere idol was not without its merits.

Protestantism's Only Missionary Martyr in Japan

Japanese Christians, however, were not the only ones arrested and imprisoned for their witness for the Lord. About the same time, in October 1941, that missionaries of the Independent Board for Presbyterian Foreign Missions and the Orthodox Presbyterian Church Mission in Manchukuo were arrested for holding that Jehovah God was the supreme sovereign, two independent, Irish brethren missionaries, R.G. Wright and John Hewitt, were picked up and imprisoned in Tokyo. Mr. Wright was put into a cell, crowded with common thieves and vagabonds off the street, and fed food so dirty he could not bring himself to touch it.

John Hewitt (back row, right), only Protestant missionary martyr in Japan. R. Wright on left.

Later that day he heard Hewitt brought into another cell, and heard him preaching the gospel to his cell mates. About ten that night, both men were released on condition that they promised to be back early in the morning for questioning. For five days they were given separately what Wright calls "the third degree," long hours of grueling questions, with relays of examiners, questions concerning what they thought of Ise Jingu, Christians bowing before shrines, the "deity" of the emperor, whether or not spirits actually dwelt in shrines like Meiji, and what the Bible taught about such things. Wright says that he tried to answer as politely as possible, and without giving unnecessary offense, but that his answers about Ise made them so angry his interrogator jumped to his feet with flushed face and flashing eyes.

After five days of this questioning, they were released. On December 8, 1941, Mr. Wright was on board a Japanese ship sailing for America but with the outbreak of war was returned to Yokohama. He attributes his being alive today to the fact that in Kanagawa Prefecture no police records were available on him. He was put into an internment camp without incident and the next year repatriated on the Tatsuda Maru.

With John Hewitt, however, it was different. He was immediately picked up on December 8 and imprisoned in Sugamo prison.[4] He had had his passage money to Ireland with him a few days before but no accounting of this has ever been given. He was in excellent health at the time but within a few weeks, by the middle of January, according to the police record later examined, he was very ill and irrational. He was sent to the Matsuzawa Byoin, Tokyo's insane asylum, but when Christians asked where he had been taken they could not find out. Finally, some days before his death, the authorities sent word to his Buddhist neighbor asking him to make preparations for a funeral for the foreigner who used to live next door. The neighbor's child overheard and told a Japanese Christian who informed two lady missionaries who had not been put into a concentration camp. Together with a third lady they went to the hospital.[5]

Secretly they were given admission and taken into the pauper ward, where they found Hewitt lying on the floor as the bed was too short for him. He was in a very weak condition but whispered, "Praise the Lord! Praise the Lord!" He seemed quite rational but could only talk in a whisper. They learned afterwards that while they were there the police had called asking if the foreigners had been admitted, but the hospital orderly who replied had denied it.

Missionary Wright states that after the war he saw the medical report which claimed Hewitt was schizophrenic, a type of psychosis characterized by loss of contact with one's environment and by disintegration of personality. The report admitted he was not dangerous, simply singing hymns under his blanket. For a number of reasons, Wright is strongly suspicious that certain experimental drugs had been tested on Hewitt and that this is the reason for the sudden deterioration of his health. The third day the three lady missionaries, and some Japanese Christian women, took turns spending the whole day with Hewitt, but that night the Lord took him Home to be with Him. When they learned the next day that a Buddhist funeral service was to be held, the ladies went to the police and got permission for Mr. Davies, one of the missionaries in the internment camp, to be released to hold a Christian funeral service also.[6]

John Hewitt, Protestant Christianity's only missionary martyr for the faith in Japan, did not die without leaving behind him a testimony to his unbending opposition to the darkness of Shintoism and to his steadfast faithfulness to his Lord. After the war, preserved with his hospital records, there was found a tract on which he had scrawled in pencil these words of Ephesians 5:11 and 12: "Have no fellowship with the unfruitful works of darkness, but rather reprove them; for it is a shame even to speak of those things which are done of them in secret." Thus ended the life of this young missionary, a godly and zealous Christian, who had left his native land to come to Japan to plead with men that they might be "turned to God from idols, to serve the living and true God; and to wait for His Son from heaven." The forces of Shintoism were able to bring him to his death very easily in 1942, but within four years they were to see the nation brought to ruin because of their foolish ideology, their own iron grip on the government broken and the doors thrown open wide to the free preaching of the Christian gospel.

———————————

1. Baker, *op. cit.*, p. 135.

2. There were others also, such as Miss K. Kitayama, whose story is told by Eric W. Gosden in his book, *Night Came to Japan*, Marshall Morgan & Scott, London, 1951, p. 65.

3. Translation of the official court charge in the possession of Mr. Yamanaka.

4. Sugamo prison, in eastern Tokyo, was the place where the Allied Powers' Japanese war criminals were incarcerated after the war and where those condemned to death were executed.

5. The Misses Esther Bower, Anne Pfaff and Grace Farnham.

6. Missionary D.E. Davies, in a letter to the *Nippon Times*, July 1951, protesting the "return of compulsory religious rites" in a government school, declared that during the war "many [Christians] made the supreme sacrifice, among them a personal friend, a missionary, because of their loyalty to Christ and refusal to compromise."

Part 3:
The Third Effort:
The Mission of
the Evangelical
Societies

8

Freedom: Christendom's Gift to Conquered Japan

"Perhaps never before did a nation whose concepts were so seasoned with Christian thought use its civil power to strike such a blow at a heathen religion."

With her unconditional surrender in August 1945, Japan, for the first time in her history, had to submit to the occupation of hordes of enemy troops. Her navy sunk, her air force destroyed and her army disbanded, she was left totally without any armaments whatsoever. Not only this, but her great wartime factories were in ruins, as were also the cities that once sheltered them and supplied their power.

"How are the mighty fallen." The words could not help but come back to the writer as he crossed Tokyo to the Imperial Palace in February 1948. In April 1941, he had traveled across the empire, from Harbin, Manchukuo, to Yokohama,

The emperor as a god, before the war, common people squatting on the ground with bowed heads.

The emperor as a man, after the war, the people standing and receiving the emperor's salute.

when it was at the top of its power. The mighty military juggernaut the Shinto militarists had built up over the years was poised for action. Defiantly the empire faced the Western powers and warned them not to interfere with Japan's expansion to the south and her destiny to rule all of Asia. Then suddenly she had struck. The Pacific naval bases of America and Britain were the victims. But now this was all over. Standing in front of the Imperial Palace's "sacred soil," before the *Nijiu Bashi* (Double Bridge), that former shrine of Emperor worshipers, one could now see armed foreign soldiers guarding the entrance! An Aussie on one side, with bayonet fixed, and an American on the other. Perhaps nothing could more adequately symbolize the death of the dream of world empire than that scene.

What startling differences there were on every side! For the first time in his life, the writer saw a damaged Shinto shrine with no one making any effort to repair it. Yet there were many of these, large ones and small, throughout the nation's destroyed cities. Courteous policemen with wooden batons instead of long swords strolled the streets. No Rising Sun flags appeared anywhere. No rousing military marches blared from the station platform loudspeakers, nor were there any little knots of people bowing farewell to straight-backed young soldiers. The military convoys rolling down the streets held white-

Stars and Stripes raised on the Imperial Plaza before the palace's Nijiu Bashi

skinned soldiers, and the occasional mighty parades that filled the wide Imperial Avenue, in front of the palace, from side to side with marching soldiers had the Stars and Stripes waving above, as did also the reviewing stand in front of the Double Bridge. Truly, it was like another world!

Perhaps never before in the history of a nation did a war and its conclusion bring such staggering changes to a people as those that came to Japan in 1945. The physical changes themselves were vast. Geographically Japan lost not only her overseas possessions but the islands to the north and south, being left with four main islands whose land area is less than that of the state of California. Of the 116 chief cities and towns, devastation from fire bombing ranged from 35 percent to 95 percent. The two largest cities, Tokyo and Osaka, were 80 percent destroyed while Nagoya, the third city, was 60 percent demolished and Hiroshima and Nagasaki almost completely so. Over 2,650,000 residences were destroyed, to say nothing of business enterprises, schools and government buildings, into this reduced housing and land area the hundreds of thousands of returning colonists

Ruins of Tokyo (Asakusa) following the air raids, August 1945

and soldiers were poured, until ten years after the war the population of the nation had passed the 89 million mark and the city of Tokyo had surpassed 8 million.

Over one-third (581) of the nation's 1,600 Protestant church buildings were destroyed and half of the Protestant schools. Some 160 Protestant churches were destroyed or damaged in Tokyo alone, leaving only five undamaged. Half of Osaka's churches were destroyed and 27 out of 30 in Yokohama. Such then were some of the tragic consequences that followed the Shinto-inspired dreams of world conquest.

Religious Freedom Comes to Japan

As staggering as were such changes, however, they were not as far reaching as those that entered the nation's life and polity. If one word were to be chosen to symbolize that change none would be more appropriate than the word "freedom." Only those who lived under the old regime can appreciate the vast difference in this regard, of life in the new Japan, with its freedom to talk, think, read, and travel as one wills. Perhaps the most dramatic statement illustrating this change comes from the pen of the emperor's younger brother, the erudite Prince Mikasa.

In the appendix of his new book on archaeology he wrote: "When I was in Nanking (as a member of the General Staff) I lost all faith that the war was a 'holy war' and wanted only peace. I was completely disgusted with the atrocities the Japanese Army committed on the Chinese people. Under the name of a 'holy war,' looting, violence, arson and rape were rampant…. I would like to apologize to my subordinates of that time concerning the fable of 'the holy war.'" And then, speaking of his return to civilian life, he said, "After the war I learned the pleasures that can be experienced by talking freely with others in a classroom.... I was freed from the shackles of an unnatural Imperial Family system to put it frankly, a prison without bars." Freedom was the greatest change. With its coming the official shackles of the Empire of Japan to restrict the expansion of the Empire of Christ were largely removed.

Some of the first to taste that freedom were the "dangerous thought" prisoners who were released shortly after the Occupation began. Among them were many Christian pastors whose ministry was resented by the "thought control" police.

Visiting Yasakuni Shrine to worship

Others who acted on the new freedom were pastors and churches who withdrew from the forced and unpleasant union with the United Church of Japan (Nihon Kirisuto Kyodan), one group of whom formed the new Reformed Church of Japan.

Of the directives of the Occupation forces that made these actions possible, none was more famous than the Shinto Directive issued from the office of the Supreme Commander Allied Powers, General Douglas MacArthur, on December 15, 1945. It specifically provided for the disestablishment of state Shinto as the national religion and declared its purpose was "to separate religion from the state, to prevent misuse of religion for political ends, and to put all religions, faiths and creeds upon exactly the same legal basis, entitled to precisely the same opportunities and protection." Here was a clear recognition that state (*Kokka*) Shinto was a religion along with its virtual prohibition. In acknowledgment of this, the two Chinese ideographs for *Kokka*, above the name of *Yasukuni Jinja* on the pillar in front of that shrine, were cemented over. The great significance for Christianity was that at long last it was to receive equal treatment with all other religions before the law.

This directive also condemned as ultranationalistic "the doctrine that the Emperor of Japan is superior to the heads of other states because of ancestry, descent, or special origin." Also, "the doctrine that the people of Japan are superior to the people of other lands because of ancestry, descent, or special origin." And, "the doctrine that the islands of Japan are superior to other lands because of divine or special origin."

It had been through the educational system that the Shinto ideology had made its greatest progress and it was now in public schools that the directive made some of the most striking changes. The reading of the Imperial Rescript on Education was banned and the ethics courses based on the divine emperor system were forbidden. *Kyujo Yohai* services, as well as

Postwar (1946) Shushin (Moral Education) textbook censored of Shinto ideology. Not much left!

the bow to the emperor's picture, were proscribed and the special building erected as repositories for the imperial portraits were removed or used for some other purpose. All god shelves and altars were taken down. The school textbooks were rewritten to remove all traces of the Shinto mythology, and compulsory visitation or bowing at the shrines was forbidden. At least one generation of youngsters was to go through the public school system without hearing mythological fiction taught as historical fact. How significant this will be for the future history of Japan time alone will tell.

Perhaps never before did a nation whose concepts were so seasoned with Christian thought use its civil power to strike such a blow at a heathen

Postwar (1946) Hokkaido Shinto shrine made over into a school house because of scarcity of buildings

religion. Yet it was done in the interests of freedom to the people whose lives had been completely tyrannized by the ruthless sponsors of that religion. Christendom's gift to the conquered was in the best traditions of Christianity. It was the gift of individual freedom to a people who had formerly spurned it and become enslaved by their military rulers. That this is a correct appraisal will be born out by the following quotations from MacArthur's historic "Orders for the Abolition of Governmental Sponsorship, Support, Perpetuation, Control, and Dissemination of State Shinto (*Kokka Shinto, Jinja Shinto*)":

1. In order to free the Japanese people from direct or indirect compulsion to believe or profess to believe in a religion or cult officially designated by the state; and, in order to lift from the Japanese people the burden of compulsory financial support of an ideology which has contributed to their war guilt, defeat, suffering, privation, and present deplorable condition; and, in order to prevent recurrence of the perversion of Shinto theory and beliefs into militaristic and ultranationalistic propaganda designed to delude the Japanese people and lead them into wars of aggression; and, in order to assist the Japanese in a rededication of their national life to building a new Japan based upon ideals of perpetual peace and democracy, it is hereby directed that:

(a) The sponsorship, support, perpetuation, control, and dissemination of Shinto by the Japanese national, prefectural, and local governments or by public officials, subordinates, and employees acting in their official capacity are prohibited and will cease immediately.

(b) All financial support from public funds and all official affiliation with Shinto and Shinto shrines are prohibited and will cease immediately....

(h) The dissemination of Shinto doctrines in any form and by any means in any educational institution supported wholly or in part by public funds is prohibited and will cease immediately.

1) All teachers' manuals and text-books now in use in any educational institution supported wholly or in part by public funds will be censored, and all Shinto doctrine will be deleted. No teachers' manual or text-book which is published in the future for use in such institutions will contain any Shinto doctrine.

2) No visits to Shinto shrines and no rites, practices, or ceremonies associated with Shinto will be conducted or sponsored by any educational institution supported wholly or in part by public funds.

(i) Circulation by the government of "The Fundamental Principles of the

National Structure" (*Kokutai no Hongi*), "The Way of the Subject" (*Shinmin no Michi*), and all similar official volumes, commentaries, interpretations, or instructions on Shinto is prohibited.

(j) The use in official writings of the terms "Greater East Asia War" (*Dai Toa Senso*), "The whole World under One Roof" (*Hakko Ichi-u*), and all other terms whose connotation in Japanese is inextricably connected with State Shinto, militarism, and ultranationalism is prohibited and will cease immediately.

(k) God-shelves (*kamidana*) and all other physical symbols of State Shinto in any office, school, institution, organization, or structure supported wholly or in part by public funds are prohibited and will be removed immediately.

(l) No official, subordinate, employee, student, citizen, or resident of Japan will be discriminated against because of his failure to profess and believe in or participate in any practice, rite, ceremony, or observance of State Shinto or of any other religion.

(m) No official of the national, prefectural, or local government, acting in his public capacity, will visit any shrine to report his assumption of office, to report on conditions of government, or to participate as a representative of government in any ceremony or observance.

There were other significant changes in the national polity also. Imperial Japan gave way to democratic Japan. The House of Peers was abolished and now only civilians can be members of the Upper and Lower Houses of Parliament. The people were declared to be sovereign and the sixteen-petaled chrysanthemum, the imperial insignia, was removed from the postage stamps, court houses, and other government possessions, for these now belonged to the people. The names and significance of the national holidays that had helped perpetuate the myth of the divine land and race were changed, while that of Kigensetsu, February 11, National Foundation Day, was dropped altogether.

The emperor came to call on the Allied commander for a precedent-shattering interview, but the most significant event of all was his proclamation on New Year's Day 1946. On that day he issued a rescript in which he declared, "The bonds between us and our countrymen have been tied together from first to last by mutual trust and affection. They do not originate in mere myth and legend. They do not have their basis in the fictitious ideas that the emperor is manifest god (*akitsu mikami*) and that the Japanese people are a race superior to other races and therefore destined to rule the world."[2] This was the final official break with the system that had enslaved the nation and made it a tool for the fulfilling of the ambitions of the Shinto-militarists. The Shinto divinities were at last, at least as far as words could effect it, excommunicated from political life.

A New Constitution Guaranteeing the People's Rights and Freedorn

The intent and accomplishments of the SCAP directives establishing democracy in Japan were gradually incorporated into various Diet-enacted laws, especially the fundamental law of the land, the new constitution. On November 3, 1946, the new constitution, with all its guarantees of freedom, was promulgated, seeming to end, as far as legal interference from government agencies is concerned, the long struggle between the two empires of church and state, Christ and state Shinto. Article 20 of the new law brought guarantees of religious freedom in the following words: "Freedom of religion is guaranteed to all. No religious organization shall receive any privileges from the State, nor exercise any political authority. No person shall be compelled to take part in any religious act, celebration, rite or practice." Thus for the first time genuine religious freedom was guaranteed the people in the national constitution.

The 28th Article of the Meiji Constitution had read, "Japanese subjects shall, within limits not prejudicial to peace and order, and not antagonistc to their duties as subjects enjoy freedom of religious belief." The trouble had been that participation in many of the rites of state Shinto, particularly for school children, had been interpreted as "their duties as subjects," with the result that the constitution did not provide protection for one who refused such participation for conscientious reasons. The unequivocal guarantee of the new constitution is in marked contrast with the old one. Now those interested in freedom have a sound basis for maintaining it for the nation, so long as they can preserve this constitution as the law of the land.

One clause in the new constitution, however, which was to have grave portent for the future, was Article 9, which reads: "Aspiring sincerely to an international peace based on justice and order, the Japanese people forever renounce war as a sovereign right of the nation and the threat or use of force as a means of settling international disputes. In order to accomplish the aim of the preceding sentence, land, sea, and air forces, as well as other war potential, will never be maintained." The impractical idealism of this pacifist clause is based on an unrealistic appraisal of the sinfulness of human nature, and ignores the fact that preparedness for self-defense is an essential factor for the preservation of freedom.

As a result a very unfortunate situation has arisen. For one thing, a dangerous precedent has been set, in the creation of the National Self-Defense Force, consisting of "land, sea and air forces," for the party in power to "reinterpret" a clause in the constitution so as to allow a course of action contrary to the spirit, if not the very letter itself, of its provisions. Further, the impractical nature of this clause, which General MacArthur had declared was not his idea but that of a political leader in Japan, now provides ultraconservatives in the government, who have long desired to see the clock turned back in some areas, with a good excuse to call for a reappraisal and revision of the constitution, which may well extend not only to Article 9 but to Article 20, and others also.

It is thus apparent once again that in Japan, as well as every other land, eternal vigilance and action is the price that must be paid for the preservation of freedom. The Christian cause has much at stake in whether or not there is any tampering with the constitution's guarantees of freedom. Protestant Christians, representing less than one half of one percent of the nation's population,[3] can have very little influence at the polls, yet any voice speaking strongly for truth and freedom will always carry weight. Great indeed, therefore, is the responsibility of the Christian citizen in new Japan.

New laws implementing the break with the past, and the guaranteed freedoms of the new constitution, were soon proposed to the Diet and gradually passed, before the end of 1951. A Radio Broadcasting Law was established breaking the old government monopoly of radio stations, making private stations and the purchase of time possible, with the result that the radio was opened for the preaching of the gospel from one end of the country to the other. A Religious Juridical Persons Law was passed in April 1951, based on the principle that all religions would receive equal treatment before the law. It stated in Article I, "This Law aims at giving legal capacity to religious organizations.... Freedom of Faith guaranteed in the Constitution must be respected in all phases of government. Therefore, no provision in this Law shall be construed as restricting any individual group, or organization from disseminating teachings, observing ceremonies and functions, and conducting other religious acts on the basis of the said guaranteed freedom."

The promulgation of the new constitution was followed by the passing of the Fundamental Law of Education. In this law, Article 9, on religious education, declares: "The attitude of religious tolerance and the position of religion in social life shall be valued in education. The schools established by the state and local public bodies shall refrain from religious education or their activities for a specified religion." Although this article may seem to leave a loophole for school authorities to require participation in "religious education or their activities" of that which is declared to be not a "specified religion," a circumstance that did indeed arise as we shall see later, yet it is to be remembered that behind this law is the constitution, the fundamental law of the land, with its statement in Article 20, "No person shall be compelled to take part in any religious act, celebration, rite or practice."

In 1948, a Habeas Corpus Act came into effect. Under the old regime one under arrest could be held in secret confinement for a year without any information on his whereabouts or condition being obtainable. The old Peace Preservation Law was also abolished and its provision that an arrested person was to be considered guilty until he had proven his innocence was reversed, bringing it into alignment with other democracies. The crushing defeat of Japan's military might had indeed brought a new day of freedom to the common man.

There was now genuine freedom of speech, which included freedom from "thought control" and the dreaded "secret police"; freedom of assembly, with the accompanying freedom from restricted travel or unwarranted interrogation or interruption; freedom from unlawful arrest or secret confinement; and freedom of worship, including the free choice of one's object of worship, freedom from prescribed participation in rites of Shinto or Buddhist origin or from enforced membership in a particular religious organization. All of these freedoms opened the door wide for the free proclamation of religious beliefs and gave an unprecedented opportunity to evangelize Japan with the Christian gospel. Nor were the Christian forces of the world slow to take advantage of it.

---

1. Prince Mikasa, "Emperors, Graves and the Common People," in the appendix, *My Recollections*, 1956, as translated by Hideo Nagase and the author. (Partial translation also in the Asahi *Evening News*, March 8, 1956.)

2. Holtom, *op. cit.*, revised edition, 1947, p. 220.

3. Under 400,000.

The Missionary Response to the Open Door

"So dismally had the boast of the Shinto-militarists—that the gods would protect the nation—fallen flat there was a general revulsion against Shintoism and a great curiosity to find out what Christianity had to offer."

The problem now is a theological one." With those significant words General Douglas MacArthur brought his speech to a close on the momentous day Japan signed the unconditional surrender terms, on the decks of the battleship *Missouri*. That MacArthur believed them to be true he soon showed by his actions as supreme commander for the Allied powers. Before the year was out, the iniquitous Religious Bodies Law was abrogated and state Shinto was disestablished. These, however, were negative actions and MacArthur well knew they would not be enough. Japan now needed to learn the Truth, the righteous principles of the Sovereign God, and to base her conduct on these just and holy standards. She needed to learn of the One who had said, "I am the way, the truth and the life; no man cometh unto the Father but by me." MacArthur, therefore, soon sent another message to his countrymen. It was a plea for ten million Bibles for Japan and for ten thousand missionaries to spread the Bible's message throughout the length and breadth of the land.

The Christians of the world, and particularly America, likewise accepted the truth of what MacArthur had said. The sudden open door in Japan, which had just been their mortal enemy where for years the gospel had been resisted and the saints persecuted, struck those who loved the Lord and His Word as presenting a tremendous challenge. To those whose hearts had been changed to compassion by the constraining love of Christ, the horrors of the recent Pacific War, and Japan's responsibility in it, only served to impress them more deeply with Japan's need for the transforming of Christ. To thousands of them, Japan suddenly became very familiar from the accounts of sons who were flying over her islands, anchoring in her harbors or standing guard duty with the Occupation forces. Many of these young men themselves, having witnessed life among a people without Christ, came clearly to see what God's will for their lives was.

The result of all these factors, and many more, was a sudden, tremendous missionary response to the challenge of Japan's open door. Within a half-dozen years, from some hundred different societies, nearly 200,000 Protestant missionaries had come to Japan, only about one-quarter of whom came from the old denominations of the previous century's effort.[1] The great majority came from new, evangelical missionary societies, most of which had come into being in the 20th century to do the work of evangelism which was no longer being done by the once great denominations into which the coldness of modernist unbelief had swept. If the period of the second missionary effort in Japan could be called that of the Protestant Denominations, being largely characterized by their work, so now could this third effort be called that of the Evangelical Societies, for their workers certainly are in the preponderance. These evangelicals, men and women who believe that the Bible is the very "Word of God, the only infallible rule of faith and practice," are for the most part young people, eager to learn the language and zealous to preach Christ as man's only Savior from sin and judgment. When the Communists swept the missionaries out of China, hundreds more came to Japan from that land. Most of these missionaries set to work to learn the language and to spread out to the distant cities, towns, and villages.

Great preaching and gospel-portion distribution campaigns were undertaken. Millions heard the gospel for the first time and claims were made of over 500,000 conversions. So dismally had the boast of the Shinto-militarists—that the gods would protect the nation—fallen flat there was a general revulsion against Shintoism and a great curiosity to find out what Christianity had to offer. A country Shinto priest told the author in 1949 that Shintoism had no more appeal for the young people and that this was the day of opportunity for the Christians. For six months he sent his sixteen-year-old son into town every Sunday to attend the missionary's church. A young woman convert in Mie Ken (now a deaconess) testified that she had turned her back on the Shinto faith when the sun goddess had been unable to protect her patron city of Ise Yamada from the fire bombs. Some villagers, in rebuke of the helpless gods of their area, cut down trees in shrine grounds for firewood, while many made no attempt to rebuild bombed shrines for five or six years after the war. The people were ready to listen to the Christian message and on every hand they flocked to hear the new missionaries. Never in its history did the Empire of Christ in Japan have such an opportunity for expansion as it did in those years.

The older denominations also, however, had missionaries to send. Eight of them, Presbyterian U.S.A., Reformed Church in America, Evangelical and Reformed, Congregational Christian, Evangelical United Brethren, Disciples of Christ, United Church of Christ, and Methodist organized the Interboard Committee for Christian work in Japan, with headquarters in New York. Within ten years this organization had sent out some 400 missionaries. The decision was made not to resume the old mission organizations but to work in full cooperation with the United Church and to help reestablish the National Christian Council. An Interboard Field Committee of ten missionaries was appointed to form a Council of Cooperation with twenty-four Japanese Kyodan members representing the church, related schools and social service agencies. One of their number has described the Kyodan as a "crowning achievement," "rendering an unsurpassed service to the nation at large."[2] This decision to work with the Kyodan, even to the point where this church "was to have the deciding and controlling voice, and the Western representatives were coming back just to fit into the picture wherever they might as helpers in a common, cooperative project,"[3] was made despite the fact of the Kyodan's wartime idolatry and omission of any public repentance for it.

Three Missionary Group Attitudes

In the postwar church, the odor of compromise was heavy upon the air. In general, there were three missionary attitudes towards it. There were those who determined that, as guests in the land, the only thing to do was to live with the smell and say nothing about it. There were others who felt that those who had allowed their garments to become soiled ought now to wash them clean and make their disassociation with the past clear. There were those also who held that the odor of the past was no particular problem of theirs since they were going to work in new territory where they thought no taint of it would come.

The missionaries of the first group worked with the Kyodan churches and co-operated with them in reestablishing the NCC. They reorganized the Fellowship of Christian Missionaries and renewed the publication of their periodical, the *Japan Christian Quarterly*. They abided by their decision to "await the initiative of the Japanese church in sending missionaries,"[4] which even meant that a furloughed missionary could not return to the field without the approval of the Council of Cooperation, though in at least one case it kept an able missionary from returning to his field.[5]

The emphasis in the work of these missionaries was what they called "the 3 Rs": relief, rehabilitation, and reconstruction. In 1948, Church World Service of the WCC shipped to Japan some 5,500,000 pounds of relief and reconstruction supplies, the value of which was listed at over $1,500,000. For the reconstruction of churches and schools some $3,500,000 was sent to Japan, enabling the rebuilding of 242 destroyed churches. The International Christian University was started in Tokyo and a campaign among the Churches of the Foreign Missions Conference of North America to raise $10,000,000 for it was launched. "It is to be international and coeducational and will seek to train Christian scholars for the faculties of the Christian schools and colleges, and leaders for the new Japan."[6] Its teachers of religion, as it was to be expected from such liberal backing, have been consistently exponents of modernist and neo-orthodox schools of thought.[7] It has been reported that, "Through the Council of Cooperation, upwards of two million dollars in gifts flows from the West each year to help rebuild, expand, and maintain Christian schools and other agencies, and to encourage special church projects or expansion and evangelism."[8] One who, in 1953, made a speaking tour of over fifty of these Christian schools in Japan has reported astonishment at the sums spent annually on these mission schools and the few Christian students in them.[9] According to the estimate of the Christian students themselves, the average of the Christians was between 5 and 10 percent, with few conversions being made. With the predominantly liberal faculties this is not unexpected.

The missionaries who held the attitude of the second group refused to work with the Kyodan or NCC and called upon Christians to separate from its apostasy. Many of them joined together to organize the Japan Bible Christian Council (JBCC) to bear testimony against apostasy and idolatrous practices in the churches, to do all they could to preserve the open door for the gospel, and for fellowship. They advanced their testimony through conferences, letters to the press, and a News Bulletin service. The *Bible Times*, an independent publication of one of their mission groups, also sought to promote this testimony through its Japanese and English editions.[10] The JBCC became officially connected with the Far East Council of Christian Churches and the International Council of Christian Churches, organizations dedicated to the same objectives. The emphasis of these missionaries has been evangelism to build new indigenous churches, and schools to train their pastors, which will evangelize their areas and resist all compromise with pagan ideology and practices. Their social service work has been largely church centered, thousands of pounds of relief clothing and food being sent by their home churches and distributed through the new ones.

The missionaries of the third attitude were largely those who organized the Evangelical Missions Association of Japan (EMAJ) for fellowship and mutual service. At the beginning, in 1948, they were connected with the National Association of Evangelicals of America but later discontinued that affiliation. Although most of them were working entirely outside of the Kyodan or NCC, their original determination was to forego making any criticism of these organizations, scattering as they were to distant points in Japan where they did not expect to come into contact or conflict with them. The inevitability of circumstance, that is, of evangelicals on the field coming into contact with the extreme liberalism of many of the Kyodan pastors, has led in recent years to an increasing tendency in the EMAJ to point out that it is different from the Kyodan and NCC, even to criticizing the Kyodan.

The EMAJ's official publication, *The Japan Harvest*, has done this,[11] although its emphasis in this regard can be expected to fluctuate with changing editorial staffs. For the most part it deals with informative articles and surveys. The NCC's invitation to evangelist Billy Graham to come to Japan in 1959 for the Centennial of Protestant Missions precipitated a division of opinion in this group. Some are strongly opposed to working with the modernist leaders of the NCC, even in such a campaign, while others, with an eye on the anticipated immediate gain rather than the principles involved, vigorously support it.

Reactions of Three Japanese Groups

Among the Japanese Christians after the war, there was a general willingness to acknowledge the sin of the state in declaring war on the West, but a great reluctance to confess the sin of the church of not resisting the state's wicked Religious Bodies Law and demands for shrine obeisance and emperor worship, *yohai*. As we have previously noted, the NCC even tried to put their compromise in a good light in 1949 by stating that their decision to avoid the martyrdom of resistance was due to "their sense of national solidarity" and to their desire to suffer together "in perseverance and sacrifice" with their anti-Christian countrymen.[12]

This reluctance was very evident among evangelical Christians also. One post-war group, the Japan Protestant Federation, composed of about a dozen independent pastors, after much urging by some missionaries passed a statement on the shrine question, although even among them there was opposition to it. Their resolution read in part: "The Federation ... does now definitely declare that all the ceremonies and rituals in connection with shrines and Emperor-worship are wholly religious, and have very easy possibilities of being linked with idolatry and therefore should be rejected by the Christians. We do indeed regret and feel the common responsibility for the poor testimony given by the Christian Churches in general in Japan during the war, and do heartily repent of all our mistakes and sins out of ignorance, weakness and of deception."[13]

Another evangelical, interdenominational organization, the Japan Evangelical Fellowship, organized in 1951 through the impetus of visiting NAE leaders, refused to adopt even this much of a statement although later urged to do so by a Tokyo pastor, Mr. Tokiwa. Pastor Tokiwa took his appeal to the church at large by publishing it in the *Kirisuto Shimbun*, the most widely read Christian news publication. It was a moving appeal but once again received but little response. In the light of the coming centennial celebrations in 1959, he said, he felt constrained to call something to the attention of his brethren for their action.

> That thing is the sin of distant worship of the Imperial Palace (*kyujo yohai*) which was practiced in churches, each Sunday during the worship service, throughout the country during the war.... I admit before God that I committed the same sin with my brethren.... Christians during such crises ought to stand up for the honor of God and defend the purity of His Church, even at the cost of their lives, and resist the orders of the Government authorities.... The Japanese churches have not indicated the slightest consciousness of their sin of idolatry which they publicly committed. Not only that, but they have neither repented nor uttered a single word of confession, as if they are forgetting everything. To make matters worse,

our (United Church's) delegates went to Ise Shrine to pay homage to the pagan's Sun Goddess. Why should we worship this "goddess"?

What must we do to receive the power of God to turn the people to God? We must return to God with heart-felt repentance, confessing our sins, asking forgiveness with humility and brokenness of heart, looking for nothing but the glory of God.... In the face of the coming centennial drive, I earnestly pray the Christian ministers will realize the truth of what I am saying and join in praying that we might have an opportune time to confess publicly the sins our churches committed in the past. I believe this is an urgent necessity to precede all centennial activities.[14]

This plea too seems to have fallen on deaf ears.

Throughout the nation itself, there was a great openness to hear the message of the returning missionaries. There was no doubt but that this new spirit was due to the crushing defeat and destruction that was the ultimate result of the way Japan had formerly chosen to go. Three hundred years earlier the nation had isolated itself from the name of Christ, and all who had contact with it, and had been punished by a backwardness so great that foreign ships could sail into her harbors and demand their will without fear of retaliation. A second time the nation had expelled the missionaries of the cross and forced the native church to become subservient to its pagan demands, and this time an utter devastation had befallen her great cities and armed forces. Now at last there had come a great willingness to hear what the Christian message really was. Even high dignitaries in the imperial household sought out missionaries for Bible instruction, and a request was sent to the Federal Council of Churches in America to recommend a Christian woman teacher for the young crown prince. How regrettable, and yet typical, that the one sent did not have a genuine understanding of the biblical message of regeneration and redemption. There was even talk of members of the imperial household becoming Christians.[15]

Decades earlier, in 1863, Dr. Hepburn, in almost prophetic terms, had intimated that he felt it would take a war to bring such openness. He wrote, "It seems to me that before the Gospel can be freely preached to this people the whole system of Government must be broken—shivered to pieces, and events all seem to foreshadow war which will be in God's hands, the rod that shall do it."[16] Eight years later he wrote, "Pity it is these rulers cannot profit by the experience and history of other nations, where the principle of freedom of conscience and religious liberty has triumphed only after long bloody wars. I fear that such will be its history here. The power of darkness will not relinquish his hold and long sway over this nation without a bloody struggle."[17] How tragically right he was!

Later, following success in the Russia-Japan war, Uemura wrote an article in which he warned: "A nation understanding 'the favor of Heaven' in a mechanical way, that is to say with the idea of a clan god protecting his own clan, deeming his natural relation to it as indissoluble, a god who will favor his people right or wrong—such a proud and ignorant nation sooner or later will come to unexpected disaster. The proud will not last long. Our greatest need today is to attain that humility of mind which comes from a real experience of the 'favor of Heaven.'"[18] How right they both were! The nation had indeed been warned, from both outside and inside sources, and the predictions had come true. Let us pray God the lesson has been learned.

---

1. *Japan Christian Yearbook*, 1958, in an article by Olaf Hansen on "Protestant Missions in Japan," states, "The missionary survey of 1957 reports a total of 2,710 Protestant missionaries currently assigned to Japan." The 1957 *Yearbook* listed 144 societies.

2. William Axling, *Japan at the Midcentury*, pp. 203, 210. Protestant Publishing Co., Tokyo, 1955.

3. Kerr, *op. cit.*, p. 152.

4. Iglehart, *op. cit.*, p. 41.

5. G.K. Chapman, missionary of the Presbyterian Church North, who could not return to his field in Hokkaido because Kyodan officials had become offended by his work and would not approve the Council of Cooperation's inviting him back to work there.

6. Kerr, *op. cit.*, p. 157.

7. Emil Brunner, Georgia Harkness, John Wick Bowman.

8. Iglehart, *op. cit.*, p. 42.

9. A member of a WCC visiting youth team that toured the Christian schools.

10. Published by the Japan Mission of the Independent Board for Presbyterian Foreign Missions in Tokyo, as a magazine, alternate months.

11. See *Japan Harvest*, Spring 1957, "Presbyterianism in Japan," by W.A. Mc-

Ilwaine, p. 15; and "Kyodan Formed Without Pressure?," by T. Tokiwa, p. 23.

12. From the report of the NCC of Japan to the IMC-WCC-sponsored conference in Bangkok, December 1949.

13. Japan Protestant Federation Bulletin, December 1951, Tokyo.

14. Mr. Tokiwa of the Reformed Church. See *The Bible Times*, No. 4, 1957.

15. See Kerr, *op. cit.*, p. 146.

16. Takaya, *op. cit.*, p. 64.

17. *Ibid.*, p. 106.

18. Aoyoshi, *op. cit.*, p. 202.

10

"The Road Back"

Within a half dozen years from the close of the war, a tapering off of the great openness towards Christianity became apparent. By the time the Peace Treaty was signed in September 1951, a very evident revival of interest in Shintoism was apparent. Shrines were repaired, the throngs attending the shrines on festival days increased and government dignitaries, including the whole cabinet, began to give the prestige of their presence to some of the famous shrines. This resurgence of interest in Shintoism increased steadily until a Tokyo newspaper could report, concerning New Year's Day 1955, "In what was unquestionably the greatest pilgrimage on record anywhere, at any time, more than 3,400,000 Japanese visited the Meiji Shrine in Tokyo on New Year's Day and yesterday. On January 1st more than 2,700,000 persons journeyed to this shrine."[1] A year later the report read, "About 3,000,000 persons in Tokyo trekked to Meiji Shrine to offer prayers for a successful and happy 1956 on New Year's Eve and New Year's Day."[2]

"In spite of all the guarantees of religious freedom, it soon became apparent that under the Shinto revival, efforts were being made by some to circumvent aspects of the new law which would seriously jeopardize religious freedom."

Missionaries noticed that crowds at street meetings and tent campaigns were not so great as before and that, in spite of the many decision cards signed, church attendances were not showing any marked increase. In the spring of 1953 a pastor wrote an article in which he cautioned, "Missionaries will see many people who raise their hands and sign decision cards at their special evangelistic meetings, but it doesn't necessarily mean they have faith.... After the war, the Pocket Testament League, Youth for Christ, Lacour Musical Evangelism, Stanley Jones and Kagawa Evangelism, plus others, made evangelistic tours all over Japan. If we added up all those reported as having made decisions for Christ, it would be a vast number. But the number of church members has not increased from before the war, for, according to the Christian News Year Book, the total was 213,700 in 1951, but in 1939 it was 222,300. Also the baptized in 1936 were 14,500 but in 1951 they were 22,500! In some groups there were many who left the churches after they were baptized. Is this not because there was a failure to bring them up in the Word after the invitation message was preached? We should consider those who sign cards as expressing their willingness to learn and we should teach them the Word of God carefully."[3]

The Old Problem

In spite of all the guarantees of religious freedom, it soon became apparent that under the Shinto revival, efforts were being made by some to circumvent aspects of the new law that would seriously jeopardize religious freedom. The effort was made in the schools and would have seriously undermined the constitutional separation of religion and state. This would have been a far step back to feudalistic concepts and government instruction of Shinto ideology, had it been successful. In the fall of 1950 the minister of education, Dr. Teiyu Amano, announced his intention of introducing an ethics course into the schools. Early in 1951 a news story was published stating, "A furor was created when the Education Minister was quoted by some journals to have said that he was thinking of reintroducing 'shushin,' the notorious prewar ethics course, into the school curriculum. Newspaper editorials as well as educators criticized the idea of reviving 'shushin' which in pre-surrender days was the 'whip' that drove Japanese school children to fanatic Emperor worship and devotion to the state."[4]

Dr. Amano prepared what he called "the People's Moral Code," based on the concepts of the old *shushin*, but opposition to it continued throughout the year. A large Japanese language newspaper editorialized, "Our past misfortunes were derived from imposition of 'morals' from the Government upon a submissive people. We must never repeat the same mistake again."[5] By November, Dr. Amano reluctantly gave in to the opposition and issued this statement: "I am willing to deal with the matter with an open mind. I cannot understand, however, why there is such opposition. When I say that the Emperor is the moral center of the nation, I mean that from him emanate all faith and love. I am only saying that he is the center of all love."[6] Thus once more the emperor was put in the place of God, which is but further evidence of how hard it is to change an individual's convictions established through decades, and how difficult it will be to change those of the old people of Japan.

Every minister of education since then has advocated the teaching of an ethics course, based on *shushin*, in the government schools. In December 1955, Education Minister Kiyose gave an interview in which he called the Occupation ejection

Ceremonial tents erected for National "Mokuto" to comfort spirits of the war dead, May 2, 1952.

of *shushin* from the schools "absurd." In February of that year the former ambassador to Greece wrote an equally startling statement to the *Nippon Times*. "When I called on [former] Premier Yoshida at Oiso last May, I emphasized the importance of respecting the two shrines in Ise and the necessity of restoring the 'Kimigayo' as the national anthem, and the Imperial Rescript on Education as the foundation of national ethics. He reminded me of the fact that when he was appointed premier he visited not only the shrines at Ise but also that of Atsuda near Nagoya. He also explained that his failure to create the textbook of national ethics was due to the resignation of the Minister of Education. I pointed out the usefulness of encouraging Christianity throughout Japan, because all civilized free states in Europe and America adopted it as the foundation of morality."[7]

On March 4, 1952, an editorial had appeared in the *Nippon Times* entitled "The Road Back," in which the following statements were made.

> The approach of Japanese independence has been unfortunately accompanied by a growing number of proposals which could readily be interpreted as pointing the way along a road back from democracy.... Recent examples have included the Education Minister's abortive attempt to foist a moral code upon the people, the proposal to revive "*Kigensetsu*" (Empire Foundation Day) based upon mythology—as a national holiday, the moves towards the standardization of the school textbooks to only those approved by the Government, and the plan to replace the popularly elected governors [School Boards] with Government appointees.... Still another measure which must be considered as pointing to a dangerous trend, is the approval given by the Diet to a resolution providing for the promotion of Oriental spirit and culture.... There is nothing wrong, of course, with having Japanese youths acquaint themselves with the spirit and culture of the Orient. But the choice of Chinese classics as the media reveals an attempt to revive the moral code based on the Confucian school of philosophy which stresses among other things the feudal lord-retainer system—the basis of Japanese militarism.... The recent proposals pointing the way back must be revealed for what they are, and an alert public opinion must keep this nation on the road toward the principles upon which the New Japan is founded.[8]

Within a year Tokutaro Kimura, head of the National Safety Agency (and as such Japan's Defense Minister with direct control of the National Safety Force and Maritime Safety Board) stated flatly that he personally favored "bringing back the pre-war Imperial Rescript on Education as a 'spiritual backbone' for members of Japan's new defense forces." The *Times*'s call for an alert public opinion to keep the nation on the right road was needed.

On the night of March 8, 1951, a group of missionaries, from seven missions working in Japan, met in Tokyo and formed the Japan Bible Christian Council. The opening sentence of the preamble to the constitution they adopted that night began: "Whereas, it is the duty of all believers in the Lord Jesus Christ to make common testimony to their faith in Him, especially in these darkening days of apostasy..." It went on to state:

Whereas, in Japan today, due to the influence of modernist missionaries and institutions on the one hand and the influence of the glorification of race, national tradition and pagan cultural practices by the Shinto-militarists on the other hand, the majority of churches and pastors have fallen into and continue to follow the way of a quasi-Christianity which regards truth as relative, the Bible as containing errors which neutralize its authority and the pagan religious customs of the ancestors as not inconsistent with Christian practice, such attitudes being notably present in the United Church of Japan (Kyodan) and the groups comprising the National Christian Council of Japan, component parts of the World Council of Churches; and

Whereas, in Japan there are pagan cultural practices which have been common occasions for Christians' stumbling, we hereby specify the following:

1) *Go-shin-ei-o-haisuru* (worship of the imperial portraits);

2) *Jinja sampai* (going to the shrines to worship);

3) *Yohai* (distant worship of: a. The sun goddess, Amaterasu Omi Kami; b. The Emperor of Japan; c. The imperial sanctuary in the palace compound which includes the (1) *Kashikodokoro* (repository of the replica of the sacred mirror in Ise Kodai Jingu); (2) *Koreiden* (god house of the imperial ancestors); (3) *Shinden* (gods of heaven and earth); (4) *Ijin suhai* (worship of great men, such as Emperor Meiji, General Nogi, Admiral Togo); 5) *Sosen suhai* (ancestor worship, such as: a. Offerings to ancestors; b. Burning of incense to the dead; c. Praying for the dead; d. Bowing before the body or the portrait at the funeral; e. Holding memorial services for the dead as practiced by the Buddhists …"

Finally, it concluded with the following: "Therefore, those forming this Council do now establish it as an agency unequivocally opposed to all forms of unbelief, idolatry and compromise with them, and unreservedly dedicated as a witness to 'the faith once for all delivered unto the saints.'"[9] Within a very few months they were called upon to make such a witness concerning the first clearcut case of a conflict between church and state under the new constitution.

---

1. *Asahi Evening News*, January 3, 1955, Tokyo.

2. *Ibid.*, January 3, 1956, Tokyo.

3. M. Goto, *The Bible Times*, April-May 1953, Vol. III, No. 4-5.

4. *Nippon Times*, January 19, 1951, Tokyo.

5. *Yomiuri Shimbun*, October 24, 1951.

6. *Nippon Times*, November 28, 1951.

7. *Ibid.*, February 19, 1955.

8. *Ibid.*, March 4, 1952, Tokyo.

9. Constitution of the JBCC, printed in pamphlet form.

11

"Sin is so close to men that much of it they do not even recognize as an offense to God, and this they need to be told."

The Conflict Is Resumed

L ate in June 1951, the following letter appeared in the *Nippon Times*.

A deplorable return to prewar State religion took place today in the schools of Japan. At 10:15 the students were ordered to "offer silent prayer" to the spirit of the Empress Dowager. (This was the time of her funeral rites.) The Christian children, who refused to disobey the true and living God by bowing their heads and praying to the spirit of the deceased, again became a spectacle before the other school children. In view of the fact that the Mino Mission suffered much persecution in prewar days because our Christians refused to participate in shrine worship, then compulsory for all schools, we are much concerned for this situation. We trust that the Ministry of Education will take steps at once to snip in the bud any compulsory religious services in the schools.

P.S. One of our Christian girls has just returned from the Tomida High School and reports that before worshipping in "silent prayer" as above mentioned, the entire school (standing in the school yard) faced toward Tokyo and at a given command bowed deeply. Upon hearing this I said, "*Kyujo Yohai*," and the girl replied, "Yes, just the same as before the war." This girl and three other Christians stayed in their classroom during this period of worship. Even if these children do not receive persecution from now on, they will no doubt be considered *hikokumin* (anti-nation and people) by the rest of the school children. I am sorry indeed that this has happened in postwar Japan.[1]

The letter was followed by an editorial note that stated,

The Ministry of Education has informed the *Nippon Times* that no instructions were issued to offer silent prayer to the late Empress Dowager. In accordance with a decision reached by the Cabinet, the schools were informed that it would be desirable if this were done. A translation of the instructions follows: To the heads of state schools ... From Daishiro Hidaka, Parliamentary Vice-Minister of Education. Re: expressing condolence on the day of the funeral of the Empress Dowager. The various central Government offices, with the understanding of the Cabinet obtained on June 12th, have decided to express condolence on June 22nd, the day of the funeral of the Empress Dowager. It is our desire that your offices and the schools under your jurisdiction will express condolence in a way similar to that in which the central Government offices will express condolence. You are asked to direct your attention to the following points.

1. The Emperor will pay tribute (*mokuto suru koto*, pray silently) at 10:20 a.m. on June 22nd.

2. It is desired that on the day of the funeral the primary schools, and junior and senior high schools, will see that the teachers, students and pupils gather and pay silent tribute (*mokuto suru koto*) and that the students and pupils listen to addresses ...[2]

The JBCC Acts

When this startling illustration of an infringement of democratic Japan's constitutional provision for separation of religion and state (accompanied by a return to emperor worship) was published, some Japan Bible Christian Council (JBCC) members immediately began an investigation. This culminated in a visit to the minister of education by the writer and a Japanese Christian, and was followed by a JBCC letter to the *Nippon Times*. The following excerpts from that letter will show something of the nature of the testimony given by the JBCC at this time.

When we of the Japan Bible Christian Council saw in your newspaper of June 26th the discussion under the heading of Freedom of Religion, we immediately acquired a copy of the official release of the Ministry of Education to the government schools concerning this matter. This states clearly that at the time (10:20 a.m., June 22nd) when the Emperor worships (*reihai suru*) the school children are to (*mokuto suru koto*), "offer silent prayer." As this seemed to be at variance with your printed statement, "The Ministry of Education has informed the *Nippon Times* that no instructions were issued to offer silent prayers to the late Empress Dowager," we have called upon the Minister of Education to discuss the matter with him. His feeling was that the use of the word *mokuto* in no way put the government in the position of calling upon the students to perform a religious rite. The Minister admitted that the word has a religious origin and we stated to him that our careful investigation revealed that the average Japanese person still interprets it as having a religious significance since it literally means "silent prayer." Thus, regardless of the intention of the Ministry's statement to the schools, it resulted in school officials calling upon students to perform acts which Christians definitely feel are of a religious character and a violation of the Second Commandment, and thereby infringed the principles of separation of Church and State, and Freedom of Religion, which are inherent principles of a true democracy. An obvious violation of these principles to us was the incident of the Tomida High School....

We have since learned that other schools throughout the nation also called upon their students to *mokuto*, and here in Tokyo, in at least one school, the faculty officially informed the students that those who did not participate would be regarded as Communist sympathizers. Although the Minister of Education declared that it was not his intention to call upon anyone to perform a religious rite, the above deplorable situation has arisen because the word used in the Ministry's released statement called upon the students, not just "to pay silent tribute" but, to pay tribute by the religious act of offering silent prayer (*mokuto*). We urged upon the Minister the need of using terminology which has no religious significance when calling upon the students to perform acts of patriotism, or respect for the dead, which would be in keeping with the principles of Freedom of Religion and would enable those of all faiths to participate. The Minister very obligingly concurred in this suggestion and agreed to discuss it in the proper committees....[3]

On July 6 and 8, numerous letters of comments were published, one of which, from a Japanese writer, bears quoting.

I agree with the Japan Bible Christian Council in the view that *mokuto* is generally interpreted as having religious significance.... To the average Japanese mind, *mokuto o sasageru* usually means "to offer silent prayer to the soul of the person or persons concerned," and accordingly it carries religious significance. A majority of the Japanese people, who may be described as generally polytheistic, will take such compulsion or persuasion as indicated in the Education Ministry notice without much fuss, but to the Christians, who jealously treasure their freedom of religion and conscience, this means a serious infringement of their moral freedom. One infringement, if left without protest, is liable to invite another, and another and another ad infinitum. Let us guard ourselves against a slip back into the prewar and wartime moral regimentation. May I remind Mr. S—, and other persons who share his view, of the fact that during the war, the Japanese Government put pressure upon Japanese Christians to revise the wording of the Prayer Book where it concerned the Emperor.[4]

On July 12, the editor closed the discussion in his Reader's Column, with the following interesting comment: "The only reason we have hesitated this long to end the Freedom of Religion controversy is that this issue caused a nation-wide furor in prewar days and unless certain basic misunderstandings are cleared up we fear that the trouble may flare up again at a less propitious time than the present."[5] His prediction of a repetition of the trouble was not long in being fulfilled.

On September 14 of the same year, another letter appeared in the *Nippon Times*, from the former Tomida writer, stating that once again the principal of the high school had ordered the students to do *mokuto*. The occasion was the celebration of the signing of the Peace Treaty in San Francisco, just concluded, and the silent prayer was to the spirits of the war dead to console them for their great sacrifice. In a second letter, on September 27, she described the circumstances thus: "Had these [Christian] students known beforehand, they most certainly would not have attended this ceremony, just as they did not attend the one in June. This time, however, no mention of a religious rite was made until all the students were assembled in the school yard for the usual Monday morning lecture and instructions. No opportunity to leave was given to those who did not want to participate. The entire group was ORDERED to offer *mokuto* in spite of the assurance given you (the *Nippon Times*) by the Tomida High School Principal that "no order of this nature was issued." Also, according to the information given you, I note that the School authorities WATCHED to see who did NOT take part in the *mokuto*. Her specific question was "whether or not the Constitution permits School authorities to ORDER students to participate in religious rites."[6]

During the next ten days a flood of letters appeared on the matter, although only a few of them were to the point or in defense of the principle of freedom involved. Finally, on the 24th, the editor closed his columns to further letters on "silent prayer," although he agreed to carry her further letter of explanation on the 27th, quoted above. One of the statements the editor made in his remarks ought to be remembered by Christians in Japan for their future use. He wrote, "If Miss Whewell or anyone else can present us with a case now or in the future where some child has been penalized in any manner for refusal to participate in *Mokuto* or a religious ceremony of any kind, we will fight with every weapon we have to defend his rights." It was his concluding question, directed to the missionaries of Japan, however, which the JBCC felt they could not allow to pass without an answer. It was this. "In summing up, would it be too much to ask missionaries—who are for the most part doing immense good in this country—not to interfere with our customs and manners?—Ed."[7]

United Evangelical Action

The officers of the JBCC prepared a mimeographed letter, addressed to the editor, which was mailed out to the evangelical missionaries of Japan for their signatures. Some 300 of them signed it in what was probably the most forthright and largely backed statement on Shintoism, and the Christian's refusal to compromise with it, ever published in Japan. It was taken to the then-president of the *Nippon Times*, a professing Christian, who agreed to request the editor to print it, and was carried on October 12, together with the names of the signers. Believing that it represents one of those times in history when the conflict between the two empires was brought to a very sharp focus, the entire letter is reproduced here.

At the conclusion of your editorial in the September 24th "Readers in Council" column you ask the following very pointed question of missionaries in Japan: "In summing up, would it be too much to ask missionaries—who are for the most part doing immense good in this country—not to interfere with our customs and manners?—Ed."This is a question we evangelical missionaries feel ought to be publicly answered, now that you have thus publicly asked it. We trust our answer does not offend you, but we must report that there are many evangelical missionaries who cannot give a blanket consent to your request, in the absolute sense in which you apparently mean it. In view of your previously demonstrated willingness to maintain freedom of the press in Japan's new democracy by publishing both sides of an issue, even when it does not coincide with your personal viewpoint, we believe you will see the justice and necessity of carrying our answer to the question you have raised in this instance.

There are many charming customs unique to Japan which have no known religious origin, and certainly we are not trying "to interfere" with such. But there are many other Japanese customs which do have a distinctly religious significance, customs which we believe keep men from God, blind their eyes to the truth and are destructive of their very souls. As the servants of Jesus Christ how can we but protest the compulsory participation of Christian believers in them? We believe that *mokuto* (silent prayer) to or for the spirits of the dead, is just such a custom and we are opposed to its reintroduction into the state schools.

What, then, is the method of our opposition, of our interference? Do we forcibly interfere? Certainly not! Our purpose is to preach the transforming gospel of our Lord, to plead with men to be reconciled to God through Jesus Christ, and to beseech them to turn from their sinful ways to the Saviour, the living and true Way. Sin is so close to men that much of it they do not even recognize as an offense to God, and this they need to be told. If men are offended when, with love and kindliness, they are told that God is displeased with idolatry and false religious customs, then it is the "offense of the cross" of Christ. That offense in the Apostle Paul's day was not only the preaching of the gospel, but the preaching of it over against the false religious beliefs of the day. The evangelical missionaries and faithful Japanese Christians today know that they cannot escape giving the offense of the cross and are ready to face it, knowing that God will win others to Himself through their witness if they are true to Him.

Another matter to which we must take exception in your editorial is your assumption that *mokuto* is a custom of nonreligious significance, and that we must accept it as such. This in spite of the many Japanese people and missionaries who have written you emphatically pointing out its religious significance. Before the war the Japanese government ruled, as you have done, that a certain practice which we consider to be distinctly religious was not to be regarded as such. In that instance the announcement was made that bowing to the State Shrines was not a religious act but merely a patriotic one. Did that declaration change the nature of the act? No more than the calling of a stick a stone would change its nature into one. Who would be in a better position to judge as to what is religious and what is not, or what is a practice in which a Christian cannot participate, than those Christians who fully endorse the complete authority and trustworthiness of the Bible, the textbook of Christianity, and have given their lives to the proclamation of its message? From every direction such have written you that *mokuto* to or for the spirits of the dead is a non-Christian religious custom, and as such for Christians to be ordered to participate in its observance is a violation both of their fundamental rights and of the new constitution. How can Christians, or for that matter free men anywhere, be indifferent to such a situation? We fail to see how the new constitution can be interpreted to permit a government agency or official to reintroduce into the state schools a compulsory religious rite, even though that rite may be a custom common to both the ancient religions of Shintoism and Buddhism.

Let it be clearly borne in mind that our plea is for non-compulsion of religious rites for any and all religious groups including Christianity. We would recognize any attempt by the state to require the participation of students in observance of Christian worship in any form equally unconstitutional. We believe that a true democracy provides that no compulsion or sponsorship by the state may be applied to any form of worship.

We are tremendously concerned at the apparent indifference to what seems to be a trend to circumvent the spirit of the new constitution, at least in regard to its provisions for the separation of religion and state. We are concerned at the ease by which this ancient religious custom of *mokuto* is being reintroduced into the government schools. We are concerned at the prime minister's reintroducing the policy of reporting matters of national moment to the Ise Shrine dedicated to *Amaterasu-omi-kami* (Sun goddess), the expenses of which, if defrayed by the government, violates the principle of separation of religion and state.

In your editorial you seem to indicate that the rise of prewar militarism was due to the fact that "the militarists utilized the Emperor as a tool." We feel that this explanation misses the real heart of the matter. It was not simply the person or office of Emperor which was used so effectively to lead the nation into war, but the Emperor garbed in the "divine" robes of Shintoism. It was the Shinto Ideology, compounded with the natural greed of men, which produced the militarists. These Shinto-militarists found their task of driving the nation into an aggressive "holy" war of expansion an easy one for the ears of the people were already prepared, through the doctrines of Shintoism, to receive the heady message that it was their destiny, as the nation of the gods, to conquer the world. Shintoism must bear its responsibility for the tragedy which befell the nation of Japan as a result of the Pacific War.

Here and there we see signs of the people of Japan being prepared for the reunion of the state to Shintoist beliefs and practices and we are concerned. Why should we wait until that reunion is consummated before we sound the alarm? We know very well that if it is consummated, freedom of religion in Japan will be lost. We are not concerned for ourselves but we are concerned about the presentation of the gospel to the Japanese people. Our request is for true religious freedom which embodies non-compulsion by the state in any and all rites and ceremonies. The revival of the old system will see religious freedom, in the true sense of the word, with its many attendant liberties and blessings, lost to the Japanese people. Therefore we plead, let these infringements and trends be corrected today before it is too late.[8]

It was signed by the four officers of the Japan Bible Christian Council and accompanied by the names of the 296 evangelical missionaries in Japan who had signed it.

The semiannual conference of the Japan Bible Christian Council met a short time after the publication of this letter. At the meeting, it was decided that the letter to the press should be followed with a direct appeal to the minister of education in the interests of preventing another occurrence of mandatory *mokuto* in the schools. Accordingly the following resolution was adopted.

"Whereas Japan's new constitution cannot be interpreted to permit a government agency or official to reintroduce into the state schools a compulsory religious rite, we respectfully submit to the Ministry of Education the following two requests: (1) That the Ministry of Education make clear to all school officials that there ought to be no compulsion to participate in any religious rite, such as *mokuto* (silent prayer); and (2) That the Ministry of Education instruct the school officials that there should be no discrimination against Christian students, who for reasons of conscience cannot participate in non-Christian religious observances or in school activities on Sunday. According to the principle of freedom of religion the individual and not the state decides whether the participation in question is a violation of conscience."[9]

Two weeks later an interview was held with the Vice-Minister of Education and the petition presented,[10] with several interesting developments taking place. For one thing, the vice minister stated that the Japanese word for religion, *shukyo*, meant a specific or sectarian religion and that *mokuto* was a general term and not the peculiar rite of any specific sect. The distinction he was maintaining was between sectarian, or organized, religion and non-sectarian religion, with the contention that the latter was not *shukyo*, that is, not religious. It was his opinion that all he was constitutionally required to do was to avoid allowing sectarian religious practices into the schools. In defense of his position, he quoted from Article IX of the Fundamental Law of Education as follows: "Religious tolerance and the position of religion in social life shall be valued in education. The schools established by the state and local public bodies shall refrain from religious education or their activities for a specified religion." It was pointed out to him, however, that this article certainly could not be interpreted out of harmony with the national constitution, the fundamental law of the land, Article 20 of which reads in part, "No person shall be compelled to take part in any religious act, celebration, rite or practice.... The State and its organs shall refrain from religious education or any religious activity."

The vice minister also indicated that since July, when JBCC members had called upon them about this matter, they had been giving it serious consideration. One contemplated solution, he stated, in order to favor Christians who considered *mokuto* a religious rite and incompatible in government schools with the new constitution's provisions, was the discontinuing of any further use of it in the schools but to call upon students to stand for *mokuso* (silent thinking or meditation) when called upon for special observances of national solemnity. No final decision had yet been reached on this, however, he added. He also insisted that the ministry had not given any special permission to the principal of the Tomida High School to hold a *mokuto* following the signing of the Peace Treaty. When shown the clipping from the newspaper stating that such permission had been sought and granted he declared that it was incorrect and that he would personally investigate the matter. No further complaints of *mokuto* in government schools have been made even though six months later the cabinet was to call for voluntary participation in a national *mokuto* by the whole nation as the Occupation ceased.

———————————

1. Miss Elizabeth Whewell, Superintendent of the Mino Mission, writing in the *Nippon Times*, June 26, 1951, Tokyo.

2. *Nippon Times*, June 26, 1951, Tokyo.

3. *Ibid.*, July 1.

4. *Ibid.*, July 12, 1951, Tokyo.

5. *Ibid.*

6. A Letter of Miss Whewell in the *Nippon Times*, September 27, 1951, Tokyo.

7. *Nippon Times*, September 24, 1951, Tokyo.

8. *Ibid.*, October 12, 1951, Tokyo.

9. Adopted by the JBCC, October 16, 1951, in Tokyo.

10. Presented by Rev. J. Newland Pfaff and the author, president and vice president respectively, of the JBCC.

12

Government Officials Revive Shrine Visitation

"The same type of Shintoism that developed following the Meiji restoration has begun to rear its head again. If it heads in the wrong direction, it may again become the standard of an ultranationalist school of thinking."

With the signing of the Peace Treaty in September the rising influence of Shintoism became increasingly apparent. One of the first published incidents of an important government official renewing the prewar custom, of reporting significant events to the deities of the former state shrines, was the visit of Finance Minister Ikeda. As plenipotentiary to the San Francisco Conference, he went to Meiji Shrine to report his coming journey and to pray for success. Immediately following the successful conclusion of the Peace Treaty, the newspapers reported Prime Minister Yoshida had announced that Secretary General Matsuda, of the Liberal Party, would go as his proxy to Ise Shrine to report to the sun goddess the signing of the Peace Treaty. Following the re-

"World's Greatest Pilgrimage" throngs Meiji Shrine on New Year's Day

lease of the JBCC letter on October 12, in which appeared the statement, "We are concerned at the Prime Minister's reintroducing the policy of reporting matters of national moment to the Ise Shrine, dedicated to Amaterasu Omi Kami," some rather contradictory denials were released.

A Mr. Fukaya, commissioner of the Religious Affairs Section of the Department of Education, announced that Mr. Matsuda "worshipped not as the representative of the Japanese people but as the leader of the Liberal party, being its General Secretary." When a reporter from the *Nippon Times* called Mr. Matsuda for comment on the JBCC reference to his trip to Ise, he replied: "I went to pay homage to the Ise Shrine recently on behalf of neither Premier Yoshida nor Mr. Yoshida in his capacity as the president of the Liberal Party. I took the trip strictly as a private individual. The trip was not paid for by the government nor the party. I am a Christian, but I consider the Ise Shrine not as a place of religion but the graveyard of our ancestor. The purpose of my trip was to report to the ancestor that Japan has successfully signed the peace treaty and that we shall from now on, as an independent nation, cooperate with the members of the group of democratic nations for our prosperity."[1]

The inconsistencies in these statements hardly need comment but they do reveal the confused thinking existing on these matters in Japan, and that the compromised Christianity of the past has only abetted it. Because there was no clear testimony of the Christian church in prewar Japan, to the effect that to bow before any shrine was a religious act of worship and as such for the Christian must be idolatry, both the secular and Christian public think there is nothing inconsistent in a Christian worshiping before a Shinto shrine. One might ask Mr. Matsuda if he believed the "deity," Amaterasu Omi Kami, died and if her body is buried at Ise. If so, what profit is there in "reporting" to a dead "deity"? Or, if he believed she was only a human ancestor (which her name belies), how, as a Christian, could he think of her spirit still inhabiting the shrine premises? Or even, how could he justify trying to communicate with the spirit of the dead, a practice so uniformly condemned in the Bible?[2] The extent of the confusion concerning the Amaterasu myth could even be demonstrated by asking if the deity were a male or female, for "she" was originally addressed as "he"!

The prime minister was to go even further, however, in reviving the shrine visitation of officials. On October 18, 1951, he announced that he would attend, with his cabinet, the fall festival of famed Yasukuni Shrine, the first such visit to be held since the end of the war. His official press release declared, "Prime Minister Yoshida's visit to the Yasukuni Shrine will not be motivated by any desire to revive Shinto as a state religion. There is no question of tying Shinto with the government as in the old days. He will be attending the ceremony in the same way that a high American official would be visiting the tomb of the Unknown Soldier."[3] The JBCC News Release No. 4,[4] in commenting on this visit, pointed out the incongruity of comparing a memorial visit to the Unknown Soldier's tomb to the visit made to Yasukuni. At the latter place, the spirits of the deceased soldiers are enshrined as deities, Shinto priests offer prayers and offerings, and the cabinet members would worship by clapping their hands to call the attention of the spirits, bowing deeply in worshipful prayer to them. The news story also stated, "There are grounds to believe the reason [for the elaborate official explanations excusing the premier's visit] is that Japan's Constitution strictly separates government and religion, and the visit of Prime Minister Yoshida to a religious shrine might be interpreted as contrary to the constitutional principle. The world has not forgotten what State Shinto did to Japan in the past and we are loath to see it revived in any form, lest the tyrannical measures prior to 1945 be again adopted as a means of conquest over free men in Japan and other Asiatic nations."

The reactions of the average Japanese to the cabinet's visit could perhaps be best reflected in an editorial in the *Jiji Shimpo* entitled, "Gratitude to the War Dead":

Not only the bereaved families of the war dead but the whole nation will be glad that the festival of Yasukuni Shrine is conducted with the attendance of the Cabinet ministers for the first time since the end of the war. It symbolizes a natural flow of national feelings to thank the spirits of the war dead, though the militaristic excess before and during the war invited the Occupation restrictions. We hope that a memorial day will be set aside for expressing thanks to the war dead. The day should be free of Shinto coloring so that even devout Christians can participate.[5]

Once again the blame for the war was put on the "militaristic excess" rather than on the Shinto ideology that fostered that "excess." When the national *mokuto* memorial day for the spirits of the war dead was held some six months later it was quite apparent what "free of Shinto coloring so that even devout Christians can participate" meant.

In addition to the action of the JBCC, there were a few other voices raised in objection to what was taking place. One of the few, if not the only church denomination to go on record with a protest against what was taking place, was the six-year-old Reformed Church of Japan. Meeting in Kobe for their sixth Synod, on October 22 and 23, 1951, they passed the following resolution:

> Be it resolved, that we make clear that all Shinto Shrines are idolatrous, and that
> we should refuse to worship them; that we should not bow to the *Kamidana*, the
> *Butsudan*, nor to any other such religious object; that we should always maintain it
> is a violation of religious liberty for officials, in their official capacity, to worship at
> Shinto Shrines, attend memorial services or other religious observances; and, that
> the members of our churches should have as a condition of acceptance, whenever
> they may become an official in a civil organization, that they will not take part in
> any of the above mentioned practices.[6]

The Emperor Resumes Public Shinto Participation

The date set for the restoration of Japan's independence and sovereignty was the night of April 28, 1952. Sometime before that, the government announced that a national war memorial celebration, to comfort the spirits of all who lost their lives in connection with the Pacific War, would be held immediately afterwards, on May 2. As a gesture to the constitution's provision for separation of religion and state, it was decided not to hold the ceremony at any of the former state shrines but in Shinjuku's famous public gardens. The government's proclamation, however, announced that it would be a *mokuto* (silent prayer) service to comfort the spirits of the war dead. They invited representatives of all provincial governments and national organizations to come to Tokyo for the occasion and called upon the whole nation to join them in *mokuto* at the same time. It was also announced that the emperor and empress would lead the ceremony, which was to be the first time since the end of the war that the emperor was publicly to lead a religious service on behalf of the public.

Prior to the event, the JBCC prepared a statement inviting Christians to set Sunday, May 4, as a special "Day of Prayer for Japan upon her regaining her national sovereignty," and urging all to warn against Christians participating in the *mokuto* service. A somewhat similar statement was prepared by the Japan Christian

Theological Seminary Japanese faculty, and three independent churches, and sent out to pastors all over Japan. The English statement said in part,

> We regret that the cabinet has chosen to make the principal act of the memorial service an act which Christians know to be a religious ceremony in which they cannot participate, namely, silent prayer to the spirits of the ancestors for the repose of the souls of the war dead. Although some may be able to construe such a service, with a *mokuto* for such a purpose, as not being "accompanied by any religious features at all," a true Christian cannot do so. To him prayer is always religious, and this silent prayer has been officially announced as being the effort of the living, by a ceremony of worshipful silent prayer, to do something to ease the discomfort of departed spirits. It is regrettable that the assurance of the new constitution, "the State and its organs shall refrain from religious education or any other religious activity," has not been more literally followed. The government's chosen method of observing the national memorial day by a *mokuto* for the spirits of the war dead now puts the Christian in the difficult position of having to refuse his government's request in order to obey his Lord.[7]

There was at least one very interesting sequel to the dispatching of these statements. Early in June a letter was received by the author from a pastor in Kagawa Ken, Shikoku, with an interesting story. When he had received the statement he acknowledged in his heart that it was right. Immediately there came to his mind the fact that the wartime-formed Prefectural Religious League, composed of Buddhists, Shintoists and Christian churches, together with the prefectural authorities and the Society for the Welfare of the Bereaved, was sponsoring, on May 24–25, a United Memorial Service of *mokuto* for the condolence of the spirits of the war dead. The service was scheduled to be held in the Gokoku Shrine of Zentsuji city, and the Christians had raised no formal objection to it. Some ten thousand representative guests had been invited to participate. The pastor decided that it was up to him to do something, although his church was no longer in the League, having severed its connections with the Kyodan some six years earlier. Through his efforts he succeeded in getting the Christian League to withdraw from the Religious League and to insert an advertisement in the *Shikoku Shimbun* (newspaper), protesting the prefecture's participation in the religious *mokuto* service at the shrine, as a violation of the constitution's religious freedom guaranteed in Article 20. This was a very encouraging report to the JBCC and the Japanese brethren who had prepared these statements.

Following the national *mokuto* service, the emperor began to make a series of pilgrimages to various famous shrines, for the first time since the end of the war. On June 3 he went to Ise and worshiped before the Inner and Outer Shrines. The press reported, "Led into the inner part of the shrine by high priests, His Majesty read aloud a report on the attainment of independence and prayed for the future happiness of the Japanese people. In the afternoon he worshipped at the Inner Shrine."[8] In July he visited Tokyo's famed Meiji Shrine, and in October he attended the autumn festival of Yasukuni Shrine to worship the spirits of the war dead. The tremendous prestige these imperial visits brought to the shrines furnished a great stimulus to the popularity of Shintoism and shrine visitation, with the result that during the next two New Year celebrations over two million people were reported to have visited the Meiji Shrine alone on each occasion.

Some very thought-provoking observations on this Shinto revival were written at this time by Professor Toshiyoshi Miyazawa of Tokyo University, in the *Bungei Shunju* magazine. The article, which he entitled "The Gods Are Not Dead," was carried in English in the *Nippon Times*, and stated in part,

> The signs of the times would seem to indicate that the eight million gods of the Shinto pantheon, who brought about the downfall of the Meiji Constitution, are not only very much alive today but bid fair to undermine the already shaky foundations of the present Constitution, too. The Meiji Constitution was founded on the premise that Japan was ruled by an unbroken line of Emperors who were descended from the Sun Goddess and who themselves were entitled to divine status as "gods incarnate." ... The new Constitution carried out a wholesale purge of the gods who had prospered for 80 years past. It was truly "the twilight of the gods." But that does not mean that the gods are dead. The Emperor, for instance, is supposed to have lost his status as a god, but he still retains traces of his former divinity.
>
> A perusal of legal promulgations contained in Government circulars will bring to one's notice the signature *GyomeiGyoji*, a term of profound respect used in place of the Emperor's name (meaning, literally, "Honorable Seal") ... since the use of the Emperor's name is considered disrespectful. Only the English translation of these circulars retains the original signature, "Hirohito." It would also seem that the clause in the Constitution forbidding State allocation of funds to a

specific religion is not being scrupulously observed. Imperial Household officials claim that the Emperor's visits to Imperial shrines are made in the capacity of a private person; this would imply that the expenses incurred are not defrayed from public funds and that all the attendants from the Chief Equerry downward pay their travelling expenses out of their own pockets. This seems rather doubtful.[9]

There were other forces also at work, however, in the phenomenal resurgence of Shintoism. One of these was the constant encouragement given it by government officials in high and low places, as we have already seen in the cases of the premier and various ministers of education. The same influence was at work in the defense forces also. The Tokyo Evening News headlined a story, "Kimura Favors Revival of Education Rescript," and stated, "A Japanese cabinet minister said Sunday he personally favors bringing back the famous prewar Imperial Rescript on Education as a 'spiritual backbone' for members of Japan's new defense forces. The Rescript, issued in 1890 by the Emperor Meiji, speaks of the Imperial Throne as 'coeval with heaven and earth,' and once had the force of the Ten Commandments for loyal Japanese. It was banned under the Occupation but has never been specifically revoked."[10] A later story indicated that when units of the Coastal Safety Force put into the Bay of Ise, they were first given a welcome by the mayor of Uji-Yamada and then marched as a group to bow before the Grand Shrines.

A story in a Tokyo newspaper gave a sidelight on how school principals were also contributing to this movement. "A principal of a private high school in Akita Prefecture has been decorating his room, and a specially constructed 'Peace Tower,' with portraits of the Emperor since the year before last. He is said to have gathered his 2,000 students in front of the tower and lectured on the Emperor's divinity on national holidays. The words he used when speaking of the Emperor were, 'The Supreme Divinity,' 'Sacred Son of Heaven' and other synonyms widely used in prewar days. In Yamanashi Prefecture, a village fire brigade is reported to have paid homage to the Emperor by bowing to the Imperial Palace on the occasion of their *Dezomeshiki* or starting ceremony this year." [11]

Another unexpected contribution to the prestige of Shintoism came from the United States Security Forces themselves. For instance, there appeared in the *Nippon Times* a picture of a U.S. officer putting a shovel of coal in a new boiler with a Shinto priest in ceremonial robes standing just back of him. Below was the following story: "Three Shinto priests last Friday dedicated the new Japan Logistical

Command boiler that will supply heat and hot water to the newly constructed 45th Division buildings nearing completion at Camp Crawford. The priests prayed to the Fire God for durability, peace and protection of the boiler. Here Maj. Walter Bosky, Regional Post Engineer, Camp Crawford, puts a shovel of coal into the new boiler following a ceremony dedicated to the Fire God while a Shinto priest looks on."[12] A number of similar joint Shinto–U.S. Army dedications of boilers and swimming pools took place in the succeeding months and years. Some raised the question of whether or not the Security Forces were not trying to bolster Shintoism as a bulwark against Communism. If this were the case, it surely was a misguided and tragic policy.

These and other factors combined, resulted in such a revival of Shintoism that one of Tokyo's newspapers could declare after New Year's Day 1955: "More than 2,700,000 Japanese Saturday made their traditional New Year's Day pilgrimage to the Meiji Shrine in Tokyo, setting a new postwar record, in what was unquestionably the greatest pilgrimage on record anywhere, at any time."[13]

The nation was not altogether without a witness against this return of officialdom to shrine visitation. When Vice President Nixon visited Japan late in 1953, the press announced that plans had been made for him "to place a wreath at the Yasukuni Shrine in return for a similar act by Crown Prince Akihito at the tomb of the American 'Unknown Soldier' at Arlington." The President of the JBCC, realizing the very serious significance of such an example, immediately wrote him a letter on behalf of the council, pointing out the great difference between the religious Shinto shrine of Yasukuni and the nonreligious tomb in Arlington. Another JBCC member also wrote a letter to the *Nippon Times* Reader's Column pointing out the same facts. To the great credit of Mr. Nixon, when these things were pointed out to him he called off the visit to Yasukuni Shrine. The news story announcing this fact read: "Wreath-Laying Plans Canceled for Nixon. Plans for Vice President Richard M. Nixon to place a wreath on a shrine dedicated to Japanese soldier dead were abandoned yesterday at a hint of protest from the American religious community here.... This shrine is for followers of the Shinto religion and is not nondenominational, as is the Arlington burial place. A letter to the *Nippon Times* protesting that it would be inappropriate for an American Vice President to make a gesture at a Shinto shrine, and the probability the issue would be taken up by the American religious leaders in Japan, resulted in the visit being canceled due to a 'tight schedule.'"[14]

Secular writers also were gravely concerned by the phenomenon of Shinto revival and were sounding their warnings. Professor Hideo Kishimoto of Tokyo University wrote in a publication early in 1953, "One notices a look of concern on the faces of the intellectuals regarding this comeback of shrines and Shintoism. People remember what the shrines were like during the wartime. The extremes of ultranationalism and of coerced Emperor worship are still too fresh in our memory.... The same type of Shintoism which developed following the Meiji restoration has begun to rear its head again. If it heads in the wrong direction, it may again become the standard of an ultranationalist school of thinking."[15] His colleague, Professor Miyazawa, from whom we quoted earlier, concluded his article with these words: "The fortunes of the gods have a direct bearing upon the destiny of the Constitution; the resurrection of the gods would mean the death of the Constitution; and signs that the gods are taking a new lease on life also imply that the foundations of the Constitution are crumbling away. It is high time that the nation took a more serious view of this situation."[16] In the years that followed the publication of that article, the situation became still more serious.

---

1. *Nippon Times*, October 12, 1951, Tokyo.

2. See Deuteronomy 18:9–12.

3. *Nippon Times*, October 17, 1951.

4. Edited by the Rev. Samuel E. Boyle, missionary in Kobe.

5. Jiji Shimpo, October 19, 1951, Tokyo. Quoted from the *Nippon Times,* October 21, 1951, Tokyo.

6. Taken from the copy given the author, submitted and translated by the Rev. S. Fujii.

7. This was mailed out to nearly 1,000 evangelical missionaries in Japan.

8. *Nippon Times,* June 4, 1952, Tokyo.

9. *Ibid.,* January 24, 1954, Tokyo.

10. *Tokyo Evening News,* January 19, 1953, Tokyo.

11. *Nippon Times*, February 2, 1954, Tokyo.

12. *Ibid.,* October 30, 1951, Tokyo.

13. *Asahi Evening News,* January 3, 1955, Tokyo.

14. *Nippon Times*, November 17, 1953, Tokyo.

15. Hideo Kishimoto, *Too Japan*, February 1953.
16. *Nippon Times*, January 24, 1954, Tokyo.

Asian Churches Protest the Shinto Revival

Whether sounding the alarm in protest would avail to check the trend or not, they knew it was their responsibility to bear witness against any return of the evil ideology that so recently had brought the churches of Christ in Asia bondage and persecution.

Τ he development of the events thus far reported was being watched by the churches of the Far East with considerable apprehension. Their suffering at the hands of the Shinto-militarists was all too vivid in their memories to be soon forgotten. At the end of November 1951, delegates from many of the evangelical churches of Asia and missionaries from twelve countries met in Manila, the Philippines, for the organizational conference of the Far Eastern Council of Christian Churches. Five attended from Japan, including one who was the first Japanese to be given a visitor's visa to enter the Philippines after the war. The feeling against the Japanese was still very high, but the reception given this pastor was truly Christian. The one who escorted him to the platform for an introduction and greetings was a Philippine pastor whose wife and children had been killed by Japanese atrocities. Many others were in the audience who had suffered the loss of wives or children, including some who had suffered imprisonment for resistance to the Japanese-Occupation-enforced United Church and for refusal to bow before Shinto shrines.

Left: Filipino president Quirino meets FECCC Japanese delegate, granted first postwar visa
Right: FECCC president Ormeo welcomed to Karuizawa Conference, August 1953,
by Nagano governor

President Quirino of the Republic posed for a picture with the Japanese pastor and took the occasion of the reception he gave the delegates to make a special speech, given wide publicity the next day, directed to Japan. Both for its generous spirit in the name of Christianity as well as its historic significance, it is worth repeating in part here. The official news release describing it stated:

In a spirit of Christian charity, President Quirino Saturday evening [December 1] said that following the example of the Lord, we cannot afford to nurture the feeling of hatred toward our neighbor, the former enemy country of Japan…. In a brief introductory remark, the Reverend McIntire, president of the International Council of Christian Churches and chairman of the convention, expressed his thanks to the President for the enjoyment of the freedom of worship in the Philippines. He also told the President that the convention has adopted a Christian Manifesto against Communism. As the delegates to the convention were presented, the President shook hands with Reverend Mitsuzo Goto. It was noted that this was the first time the President personally greeted a Japanese since the last World War. Mr. Goto is the first Japanese to stay in Manila for more than 24 hours since the war.

With regard to his attitude toward Japan, the President said that inasmuch as the Lord has put us together geographically and our people will live together and our children and our children's children will some day come side by side again, he did not "want our children to inherit the hate that had been temporarily conceived in those days of torture and in those dark days before the liberation of the Philippines." ... "I have been waiting for an opportunity to express our friendship to Japan as well as to others who had cooperated with her during those bloody times," the President said.... The President added: "I want to assure our friends, especially those from Japan, following the example of the Lord, we cannot afford to nurture for an indefinite period that feeling of hate, that feeling of resentment, that negative spirit towards our neighbors because as long as we believe that there is a Power on high, we elevate all those offerings of nobility and dignity of our people so that the Japanese people can be sure that as far as we are concerned, and in the name of the future of the Filipino people, there is nothing to fear of that spirit of revenge on the part of the Filipinos."[2]

FECCC Manila Conference Expresses Concern

This FECCC Conference of Christians discussed the developing trend of the return to Shinto ideology in Japan and passed the following resolution expressing their concern:

FECCC Manila Conference, December 1951

We, the Conference of Christian Churches in Asia, meeting in Manila this 29th day of November, 1951, as an assemblage of native ministers and foreign missionaries from eleven Far Eastern countries and the United States, do hereby unanimously adopt the following resolution:

WHEREAS, there is evidence of the Minister of Education in Japan allowing and sponsoring Shinto and Buddhist forms of religious acts, such as "*mokuto*" (silent prayer to or for the spirits of the dead) in the government schools of Japan, and contending that these are nonreligious acts because they are not of a specific, sectarian nature; and

WHEREAS, the Constitution of Japan under Article 20 declares that "the state and its organs shall refrain from religious education or any other religious activity";

Be it therefore resolved, that we urge the Ministry of Education in Japan to uphold the spirit and letter of the new constitution, under which the Japanese people have enjoyed full democratic freedom, by prohibiting Government sponsored religious activity in state public schools, and thereby immediately halt the present trend.[3]

Copies of this statement were sent to the prime minister of Japan and the minister of education, as well as released to the press and quoted in newspapers in Japan.

The FECCC also expressed its grave concern at the U.S. Army's participation in Shinto ceremonies. A resolution was passed which referred to General MacArthur's directive separating religion and state in Japan and then went on to declare,

Whereas, it is common knowledge that it was the false ideology of Shintoism which enslaved the minds of the Japanese people and drove them to seek to enslave the whole Far East and bring it under their suzerainty; and, Whereas, it is generally believed that it was the combination of Shintoism with the military uniform which brought death and destruction to the Far East; and, Whereas, a news release of October 30, 1951 [with a United States Army photograph], related the story of officers of the Occupation of the Allied Powers of Japan in Cooperation with Japanese Shinto priests in the dedication of heating equipment for United States Army installations of the 45th Division to the Shinto Fire God, and

Whereas, it is our considered belief that the Occupation by thus publicly displaying this cooperation between the Occupation of the Allied Powers and Shinto worship is raising in the minds of Christians throughout Asia the question as to whether the Allied Powers, having allegedly used the Japanese Emperor to gain the co-operation of the Japanese people, is now attempting to use the Sun Goddess (Amaterasu-OmiKami) and other Shinto deities to further consolidate that friendship;

Therefore, be it resolved, that we strongly feel we must call attention to this action of the Armies of Occupation of the Allied Powers of Japan, because we feel that such a policy, if continued, will have the gravest of irreparable consequences, and we do respectfully request that all such joint services with Shinto priests be discontinued.[4]

In Japan the *Nippon Times* gave it a half-column story under the headline "Clerics Call for End to SCAP Cooperation With Shintoism."[5]

Karuizawa Conference Appeals to Education Minister

Two years later the FECCC met in Karuizawa, Japan, for its second conference, with delegates present from eleven Far Eastern countries. The report on Japan brought to their attention the increasing reactionary trend, and in the discussion that followed the decision was reached to send a communication to the minister of education concerning the press reports that the ministry was contemplating restoring the MacArthur-banned Imperial Rescript on Education to the educational system. The letter sent read as follows:

Your Excellency:

The Far Eastern Council of Christian Churches, meeting in its second biennial conference, July 26 to August 2, 1953, with delegates from Japan, China, Formosa, Hongkong, The Philippines, Indonesia, Singapore, Australia, New Zealand, Thailand and India, would respectfully extend to you and your honorable government our greetings.

We have enjoyed the most excellent hospitality of your countrymen, and the officials of Nagano and Karuizawa have given our conference their kindest welcome. When we remember that only a few years ago we were engaged in a bitter, costly war, it is with deep gratitude to God that we rejoice together in this mutual peace.

Yet our conference delegates have been disturbed by the report that there is a desire among some leaders in Japan to revive the "Imperial Rescript on Education," which was formerly the basis of Japanese school education. We are deeply sympathetic with the need for moral ideals and discipline among the postwar youth of all nations, and appreciate the desire of your Excellency to seek a remedy for the unsettled conditions among Japanese youth as a result of the recent war.

Our conference would most respectfully beg the guarantees of the present Constitution of Japan, in which it is stated in Articles 19, 20, 23, and 89: "freedom of thought and conscience shall not be violated." Freedom of religion is guaranteed to all. "No religious organization shall receive any privileges from the State, nor exercise any political authority." "No person shall be compelled to take part in any religious act, celebration, rite or practice." "The State and its organs shall refrain from religious education or any other religious activity." "No public money or other property shall be expended or appropriated for the use, benefit or maintenance of any religious institution or association or for any charitable, educational or benevolent enterprises not under the control of the public authority."

If the "Imperial Rescript on Education" should be revived and made compulsory again in all Japanese schools, the above articles of the Constitution would then be made null and void. This is quite evident when we read the "Imperial Rescript on Education. [Here the Rescript was quoted.]

Your Excellency, as Christians from the many Far Eastern countries we wish to state, humbly but earnestly, that we are of the deepest conviction that a reintroduction into the Japanese educational system of the philosophy of this Rescript, with its concept of the imperial line being "coequal with heaven and earth," is fraught with the gravest dangers for the future freedom of the Japanese people and the Christian Churches of Japan, and would involve the State in the propagating of religious concepts. We humbly submit our united request that the Ministry of Education protect the religious freedom now guaranted by the Constitution by opposing the establishment of any religion or religious organization, or propagating the concepts of such, as the compulsory basis of the State education program in Japan.

Christian children in the schools of Japan believe in the Triune God, Creator of all the universe, whose will for all nations is revealed in the Word of God. They cannot therefore accept any religious teaching in school which interferes with their supreme spiritual allegiance to Christ the Son of God, and Saviour. Because of this spiritual situation, we plead with you, Honoured Minister, to maintain the present Constitution, which is fair and just to all religions in Japan and enables our Christian brethren to be obedient and faithful subjects of their Emperor as King, to serve their fatherland with humility and patriotic loyalty, and to pray for the blessing of God on the people of Japan in their struggle to regain their place in the peaceful fellowship of nations in Asia.

As Christians we would like to add that we are of the deepest conviction that the only hope of transforming and lifting up the youth of nations to the highest standards of moral behaviour, does not lie in any Government's educational appeal to them to be good for the sake of a human leader, no matter how noble and lofty his position, but is rather in the voluntary yielding of their lives to the service of the living God through His Son, the Lord Jesus Christ. It is the duty and privilege of their parents and the Christian Churches to bring to the youth this message.[6]

Singapore Conference Speaks for Freedom

The concern of the Christians in the churches throughout Asia at the resurgence of Shintoist influence in the government of Japan continued. It came to expression again at the third biennial convention of the FECCC, held in Singapore the summer of 1956. There, as the matter was discussed, it was decided to prepare a pointed resolution and send it to the prime minister of Japan and the minister of education, as well as release it for publication. Called "Developing Threats to Religious Freedom in Japan," the resolution follows:

Above: FECCC Singapore Conference, August 1956

Whereas, in contrast to the very stern terms agreed to by the Japanese Government at the signing of the surrender of September, 1945, the terms of the Treaty of Peace offered Japan in San Francisco in 1951 by the United Nations, including many Asian countries once occupied by Japanese forces, were very generous, asking for no guarantees from Japan of a major and permanent nature other than that she maintain peaceful intentions, assuming that the new, democratic Constitution, together with the new laws implementing the various freedoms guaranteed in the Constitution, would be sufficient assurance that the objectives of the Treaty of Peace, of a democratic and peaceful Japan, would be maintained; and, whereas, there has been recent agitation in Japanese Government circles for the revision of the new Constitution coupled with the revision of the Education Law in June, 1956, which revision has been described by leading Japanese educators and Tokyo professors as indicating 'a return to totalitarianism in the field of education; and

Whereas, the Minister of Education has recently issued a statement declaring it was all right for principals of Government schools "to make their students bow toward the direction of the Emperor's Palace on national holidays," which act of *Kyujo Yohai* (distant worship towards the palace) in pre-surrender days was the focal point of severe persecution of Christians who would not participate in this form of polytheistic worship, which persecution extended throughout the Asian countries wherever the Japanese forces went; and, whereas, the revival of this mandatory student bowing again puts in jeopardy the religious freedom of every Christian student in a Government school and restores the Emperor to the position of an object of worship, thereby greatly encouraging those who seek to elevate him again to deity that they might arrogate to themselves absolute powers in the name of the divine Emperor;

Be it therefore resolved, that the Third General Assembly of the Far Eastern Council of Christian Churches meeting in Singapore this August 5 to 12, 1956, express to the Prime Minister of Japan and the Minister of Education their deep concern and alarm at these developments, urging specifically that in any projected revision of the new Constitution the guarantees of freedom of religion and of the Emperor as a human symbol of state be unchanged, and that the Minister of Education's approval of mandatory student bowing to the imperial palace be rescinded; and, be it further resolved, that we point out to the Japanese Government the fact that such developments as those indicated above will do great damage to the prestige of new Japan in the eyes of freedom-loving countries of Asia and the world.[7]

The brethren of the churches of Asia were determined that the nation of Japan would not be subjected to the control of Shinto ideology without their protest. Whether sounding the alarm in protest would avail to check the trend or not, they knew it was their responsibility to bear witness against any return of the evil ideology which so recently had brought the churches of Christ in Asia bondage and persecution. The extent of the results must await the revelation of the Judgment Day.

---

1. Mitsuzo Goto, J. Newland Pfaff, Samuel E. Boyle, Timothy Pietsch, and the author.

2. Minutes of the First General Assembly of the Far Eastern Council of Christian Churches, Nov. 25–Dec. 2. 1951, Manila, Philippines, p. 36.

3. *Ibid.*, pp. 15-6.

4. *Ibid.*, p. 10.

5. *Nippon Times*, November 28, 1951, Tokyo.

6. Minutes of Proceedings, Second General Assembly of the Far Eastern Council of Christian Churches, July 26–Aug. 2, 1953, Karuizawa, Japan, p. 35.

7. *The Bible Times*, Vol. VI, No. 5, 1956, p. 18.

14

"God opened the door in a new way for getting the gospel to this great nation after World War II. He can hold open the door of opportunity and in this the Christian can rejoice."

Voices for Freedom

In December 1954, a political upheaval brought a new premier, Prime Minister Hatoyama, into power. Shortly afterwards a release came from his office that was to bring comment and criticism from around the world. It stated that on the first of the year he would make the pilgrimage to distant Ise, as prewar premiers had done, to report to the sun godess that he had assumed the high office of the premiership. Following his sojourn, *Time* magazine described the event in these words: "Hatoyama is the first Prime Minister to make the pilgrimage since the Japanese surrender; he did so in defiance of Article 20 of the MacArthur constitution, which lays down that 'the state and its organs shall refrain from ... religious activity.' ... The partially crippled Hatoyama hobbled painfully up to a white altar at the entrance of the shrine, closed his eyes, bowed his head and paid

Prime Minister Hatoyama worships the sun goddess at Ise Shrine

silent attention to the sun goddess—and, in so doing, paid heed also to the votes of Japanese nationalists in the forthcoming general elections."[1]

When asked why he went, the prime minister replied, "As a renovation of popular sentiment," and he added that he had prayed for a prosperous harvest for the new year.

Reactions to Premier's Ise Worship

In view of the wide newspaper publicity, given shortly before, to the effect that the new prime minister was a "baptized Christian,"[2] who with his wife loved to sing hymns, the JBCC felt that if the public were not to be left with the impression that such polytheistic worship was quite compatible with Christian life, it was of the utmost importance that some Christian body should make a public pronouncement on this matter. It was their conviction that the very failure of such a witness to reach the public through the press and the churches in the past was one of the principal reasons for the establishment of the general assumption that Christians could participate in polytheistic ceremonies and that it was only extremists, who did not represent the real Christian opinion, who would not do so. An assumption of that kind, if allowed to continue, could be a great peril to the postwar unrestricted opportunity for preaching the gospel, free from government pressure to compromise with polytheism. Accordingly, the JBCC president prepared and sent to the press the following letter that was carried by the four English language dailies.[3]

> It is with much sorrow of heart that we have read the recent stories in your newspaper of the Prime Minister reintroducing the Shinto tradition of prime ministers making the long pilgrimage to Ise Jingu to report, to the mythological "Sun Goddess" worshipped there, that they have acceded to this high office. As Christians, we deplore the example and utter inconsistency of one who has received baptism as a Christian and who professes belief in the one true God of the Christian Faith and His Ten Commandments, acknowledging presence of a Shinto deity and worshipping it.
>
> The Decalogue begins with the injunction, "I am the Lord thy God.... Thou shalt have no other gods before me.... Thou shalt not bow down thyself to them, nor serve them: for I the Lord thy God am a jealous God, visiting the inquity of the fathers upon the children unto the third and fourth generation of them that

hate me; and showing mercy unto thousands of them that love me, and keep my commandments." When Japan is so desperately in need of Christian example and virtue, for one who professes to be a Christian and is elevated to the highest governmental post, deliberately to break the one commandment with which is associated the specific curse of God is truly calamitous. It is to be hoped that the Prime Minister will truly repent of this ill advised action and take no more part in such compromise of Christian principles and confusion of the new Constitution's clear separation between religion and state.[4]

How greatly the Shinto gods have confused the church in Japan can be seen in the various reactions to the publication of this letter. Although the majority of evangelicals agreed with its content, some thought it an unwise action, or even improper. The leading churchmen polled by one newspaper gave such opinions as the following:[5] "What he [Hatoyama] did is patriotic and normal for a national leader or citizen," one Christian leader stated. "As Prime Minister he is following a Japanese custom, although he may be reverting to prewar times," was the reply of "a prominent Nonchurch (*Mukyokai*) Japanese Christian." The news story also added, "Mr. Hatoyama's secretary told the Asahi Evening News yesterday that Mr. Hatoyama was baptized in his school days but is not a Christian now. He explained that he has heard the Prime Minister say that he wants to believe in God but cannot become a firm believer in the Almighty like a Christian but added that he often says that his spirits are buoyed when he sings Christian hymns."

It was, however, in an American evangelical periodical that the most unexpected comment of all was made.[6] There it was suggested that the prime minister's "act of homage" at Ise, that is, his obeisance and prayer to the sun goddess before the altar of her shrine, might be compared to the Western salute to the flag and thus construed as a "matter [that] seems to be an individual one, left squarely up to the conscience of each man." Here indeed was a new advocate for the right of Christian participation in polytheistic practices! It was by just such arguments in the past that Shinto rites gained an entrance into the churches and smothered spiritual life in idolatrous compromise. The JBCC felt that for the sake of the whole Christian cause in Japan a statement should be prepared pointing out the difference between a salute to the flag and a bow before a polytheistic Shinto shrine and accordingly a release was issued, from which the following excerpts are taken:

The Bible Council is constrained to point out why paying homage at Ise Shrine is not to be compared to saluting the flag: (1) Ise is called a *Jingu* (god house); no one refers to the flag as a god. (2) There are no religious priests attending the flag with religious ceremonies, but these are always present at Ise Shrine where priests regularly perform rites such as waving the holy *sakaki* tree to drive away evil spirits, making prayers and offering food and wine. (3) No sacerdotal offerings of any kind are made to the flag, but these are regularly made to the enshrined "deity" of Ise. (4) One is expected to wash hands and mouth in a ceremony symbolizing purification of mind and body at Ise; there is no such religious preface to a flag salute. (5) At Ise worship is rendered the so-called sun-goddess, with prayers made to her. No such is rendered the flag. (6) The sun-goddess receives a bow; the flag receives a salute. The Bible prohibits a bow to anything except God or living beings who can return the bow. Nothing is said about a salute.

Shadrach, Meshach and Abednego (Daniel 3) preferred death to the external act of bowing to an idol even though they did not believe any spirit or deity was in the idol. At Ise Shrine, men, moved by their vain imaginations, have enshrined a mirror as the material representation of their invisible, mythological deity, who is as real to them as any visible being, and before her sacred house, abode of this mirror, they bow in reverent worship to pray for blessing. It seems to us that these considerations should make it self-evident to Christians that Ise Shrine is a place of idolatrous demon worship (1 Cor. 10:29), and that none can go there to do obeisance without breaking the second commandment. (Paul wrote, "the things which the Gentiles sacrifice, they sacrifice to demons, and not to God.") Participation in any ceremony of polytheistic worship, even under the guise of culture or patriotism, can never be justified in the light of the commandments of God.[7]

The NCC Issues a Statement

The National Christian Council of Japan also issued a statement about government officials paying homage at religious shrines. In introducing their resolution, the annual Japan Christian Yearbook for 1956, "published under the auspices of the Fellowship of Christian Missionaries in cooperation with the Japan National Christian Council," stated the following: "The Japan Bible Christian Council has repeatedly protested publicly against these violations of the constitution. However, since the JBCC is a minority group with strong (American) missionary initiative, these outspoken protests have created a good deal of antagonism rather than achieving their real purpose. The National Christian Council of Japan, on the other hand, is in a better position to speak on behalf of the Protestant Church of Japan. It was with gratitude that we read of the resolution passed at the NCC annual meeting: 'In censure of government officials who pay homage at religious shrines and are considering rebuilding national shrines, the NCC resolved that religious freedom must be preserved as stated in the Constitution.'"[8]

One could well ask the Yearbook writer why he thinks a forthright testimony against church or state officials participating in polytheistic worship would not produce "antagonism," and what the evidence is that the JBCC members are not "achieving their real purpose" and that the NCC is more likely to do so. Because of the NCC's long record of vacillation and compromise on the Shinto problem, as has previously been shown, government officials may well wonder if this truly represents their spontaneous convictions on the matter, or whether at a later date, as twenty years ago, another expression might be forthcoming from them. As we have already seen, the NCC in 1930 declared, "To treat the Shinto shrines, which from of old have been religious, as nonreligious has been unreasonable." Then in 1936, they reversed this. The FECCC in Karuizawa in 1953, warning of the nature of the NCC of Japan, issued the following statement:

> The National Christian Council of Japan failed to maintain the historic Protestant position during the period of state pressure in Japan, and actually yielded in November 1936, with this official declaration: "We accept the definition of the government that the Shinto Shrine is nonreligious." Under that compromise the National Christian Council collaborated in a sinful way with Shintoism by publishing many propaganda pamphlets and by widespread *hoben* or accommodation to the totalitarian principles of the military state. This National Council is an affiliate of the World Council of Churches and shares all the defects of that organization. We advise all in Asian churches who are receiving advance publicity regarding this 100th anniversary meeting to realize the nature of the agency which proposes to celebrate Protestantism's entry into Japan.[9]

Why has the NCC been so long silent on this matter? Why has it not to this day made any public repudiation of its 1936 declaration nor any apology for it? Why, if it has had any change of heart or mind on the nature of a Shinto shrine, did the report, submitted by its delegation to the WCC Bangkok conference in

1949, defend its prewar activity rather than apologize for it? If the NCC still believes that Shinto shrines are nonreligious, why does it now protest the prime minister's attendance? If, on the other hand, they believe the shrines are really religious places, why do they not publicly repudiate and repent for the terrible compromise with Shintoism before the war? From 1932 to 1939, Dr. Akira Ebisawa was general secretary of the NCC, and again from 1948 to 1955. During the prewar period Ebisawa was the church's most vociferous propagandist for the position of the Shinto-militarists, declaring in his pamphlets that the ideology of the slogan *hako ichiu* "coincides spontaneously with the fundamental faith of Christianity," and that this "basis of the Japanese spirit" was the equivalent of "the Christian conception of the Kingdom of God." In spite of this tragic record, he was restored to office in 1948 and chosen by the NCC to be the official historian of Protestantism's 100 years in Japan! What kind of treatment of those crucial prewar years can be expected in the history written by one holding such un-Protestant views? Will there be any repudiation of the great betrayal as the church leaders faced the Shinto problem, or any just presentation of the faithful ones, both in Japan and Korea, who rejected the NCC's position and upheld the faith, even to imprisonment? It seems a travesty to give the writing of the history of the Protestant church of Japan to one who has shown such a dismal misunderstanding of the nature of true Protestant Christianity. When one takes these things into consideration, it would seem to be clear that it is the JBCC, because of the consistency of its convictions, rather than the NCC, which "is in better position to speak in behalf of the Protestant Church of Japan."

The State Turns Towards the Road Back

The first six months of 1956 illustrated further the ominous trend to what the newspapers referred to as "the reverse course." One example of this was the spring announcement that two bills were to be submitted to the Diet, one from each political party, to return Yasukuni Shrine, the former state shrine in which the spirits of the war dead are enshrined, to the support of the national treasury as a state shrine. General MacArthur's Shinto directive had forbidden compulsory worship of this or any other shrine, or the support of them with state funds, and similar proscriptions are in the new constitution. Yet in March the press reported, "Two identical plans to reorganize the Yasukuni Shrine in Tokyo into a nonreligious memorial organization financed by the State will shortly be introduced in the Diet.

The Yasukuni Shrine is dedicated to the spirits of patriots and soldiers who died in battle, The plans have been drafted by the ruling Liberal-Democratic Party and the Socialist Party."[10]

Although these plans spoke of making the shrine "a nonreligious memorial," neither envisioned the removal of the Shinto priests, ceremonies or symbols from the shrine premises. Yet the reason why the plan was quietly dropped was because of the opposition of the shrine officials themselves. The chief priest reported to the press, "It is undesirable for us to be supervised by the government in all things. I do not want to have the 'divine character' of the Shrine changed.... The chief reason for the existence of Yasukuni Shrine is to invite the wandering spirits to assemble here, and to comfort the families of the war dead."[11]

Yasukuni Shrine is apparently quite conscious that if it only waits long enough it will not have to make any changes to be restored to recognition as the nation's war memorial. If a nonreligious war memorial is not established, and there is no desire for one on the part of the vast majority, Yasukuni will get national war memorial status by default. The shrine can well anticipate that the day of support from state funds will not be far away either. Under such circumstances, we can expect when school children are taken to visit the shrine on one of their expeditions to Tokyo, that again they will be told to bow before it, and if any Christians among them should refuse, that again they will have the dread charge of *hikokumin* (haters of the nation and people) hurled at them, the most feared and abhorred charge that can be hurled against a Japanese.

A further illustration of the trend away from democratic government is to be seen in the whole course of events which took place in the Diet in the spring of 1956. A staff writer for a Tokyo newspaper wrote the following description of the situation.

> Government policies continue to be firmly focused on the recentralization of all power in the hands of the ruling groups. Already control of the Cabinet, the armed forces and police are concentrated in the hands of the Prime Minister (which means the ruling party). Control of education (and the thought processes of the young) and perhaps of broadcasting will follow.... Revision of the Constitution will almost certainly eventually take place because such a step will be successfully associated with group patriotism—and the majority will not take the responsibility of voting against the group but will accept the verdict of the ruling caste and hope for the best.[12]

The forecast concerning the education law came true on the night of June 2 when the bill to revise the Fundamental Education Law was passed in the Upper House amid scenes of rioting. The bill had been branded by the opposition as one intended to make "the educational system a tool in the hands of the ruling party," and ten leading university presidents had declared that "the proposed educational reform bill smacks of a return to totalitarianism in the field of education." [13] In order to get the bill passed before the deadline for adjournment was reached, the government had finally to call in 500 special police to restrain the opposition and keep them from preventing a vote being taken by forceful means. In the tactics used by both parties, leading to this riot in the Diet, democracy was the chief loser. The forecast concerning revision of the Broadcasting Bill is still unfulfilled although the Asahi has reported that one is pending which "would mean direct control of the Corporation and its programs by the Government." Likewise, the prediction that the new constitution would eventually be revised is as yet unfulfilled as the national election of the Upper House on July 8 failed to give the government the two-thirds majority it needed to accomplish this revision. If a revision involving the basic principles of religious freedom and separation of religion and state is not to take place, it would seem that the lovers of freedom will have to be more active than they have been in the past.

Perhaps the most glaring illustration of all of the "reverse course," however, is the one which came from the office of Minister of Education Kiyose. Since the end of the Occupation, ministers of education have almost consistently been older men of reactionary tendencies. Of none was this more true than of Ichiro Kiyose, a man whose thinking seems to be in the prewar feudalistic era. Following the war he had been the chief lawyer for the defense at the war crimes trial of General Tojo. When he assumed office as education minister he gave an interview to the *Jinja Shimpo* (Shrine News) in which he advocated a restoration of the banished *shushin* (presurrender ethics course based on Shinto ideology) in the schools. And he added, "I am very sorry for the Shrines (*Jinja*). Personally I do not think that the Shrines necessarily are religious (*shukyo*). I think that Shrine worship is but the beautiful expression of the Japanese people's ancestor worship." [14]

The next spring the newspapers reported an even more startling and reactionary statement from Minister Kiyose, one which seemed to be in clear violation of the constitution's provision guaranteeing freedom from compulsion to perform a religious act. According to the *Nippon Times* of that date, "Education Minister Ichiro Kiyose said yesterday, 'It is perfectly all right for schools to make their students bow toward the direction of the Emperor's palace on national holidays,' Kyodo reports. An Education Vice-Minister notification, dated May 14, 1947, forbids bowing toward the Imperial Palace (*Kyujo Yohai*) and shouting three cheers for the Emperor (*Banzai*), indispensable parts of holiday ceremonies at schools for the past couple of decades before the surrender. Kiyose admitted that the no-bowing order is still in effect. 'But the regulation was made on orders of the Occupation authorities and we needn't be too scrupulous about it as long as we act within our common sense,' he said. On the Emperor's birthday last Sunday, quite a number of schools were reported to have ordered their students to bow together toward the Palace."[15]

The JBCC Speaks for Religious Liberty

In view of the shocking nature of this pronouncement, the JBCC felt it could not maintain silence on this matter nor that of the Yasukuni plan. Accordingly the following letter was prepared for the press and, although delayed in its final preparation, was published on July 30 in the *Mainichi*:

Dear Sir: In three more years Protestants in Japan and the world will be celebrating the re-opening of Japan to Christianity in 1859. No doubt this one Hundredth Anniversary will bring foreign visitors to Japan and in a real sense draw the attention of world Christianity to this nation during the celebration of this important event. We are happy to express our gratitude to the people of Japan for courtesies shown to Christians during the past century, and especially to thank the Government of Japan for the excellent religious freedom which all people have enjoyed here since the war.

It is this very appreciation, indeed, which prompts us to call attention publicly to certain trends in political circles which seem to threaten the continued enjoyment of these religious liberties. It is our hope that our statement may in some measure aid the people of Japan to keep inviolable the precious right of freedom of religion which is now guaranteed so clearly by the Constitution of Japan. One alarming evidence of this reactionary trend was the agitation from some quarters to make the Yasukuni Jinja, famous Shinto military shrine, a so-called nonreligious war memorial for the nation. Although unexpected opinion developed in time to defeat this effort in the last session of the Diet, the danger remains and we respectfully register our protest against such a mistaken plan.

Yasukuni Jinja has priests, prayers for the dead, enshrinement of the dead as *kami*, and other ceremonies which are exclusively expressions of the beliefs and practices of the Shinto religion. If this Shinto place of worship should ever be made the official, state-supported war memorial for the military dead of Japan, the action would be grave injustice to all non-Shinto tax payers of Japan who thus would be taxed to support a place of worship for a religion in which they cannot believe. It also would work an injustice on the non-Shinto dead whose enshrinement in a Shinto shrine could not be in accord with their wishes.

We especially deplore the revival of the careless use of the words "nonreligious" for that which is obviously quite religious. This reminds Christians only too well of the propaganda double-talk prior to 1945 by which even bowing to a Shinto shrine was declared to be "nonreligious." Actually, such language cannot bear serious inspection. Christians consider the custom of bowing to shrines, or making distant bows toward the Palace, and all such things as religious acts in violation of God's Commandment: "Thou shalt not make unto thee a graven image, nor any likeness of anything that is in heaven above, or that is in the earth beneath, or that is in the water under the earth; Thou Shalt Not Bow Thyself To Them, Nor Serve Them; for I Jehovah thy God am a jealous God, visiting the iniquity of the fathers upon the children, unto the third and fourth generation of them that hate me, and showing loving kindness unto thousands of them that love me and keep my commandments." Exodus 20:5-6. If there is to be a really nonreligious war memorial for Japan it should be totally separate from any established place of worship under any religious organization. Only thus can the Constitution be truly obeyed and the religious liberty of the Japanese people safeguarded.

An even greater cause for concern was a statement by Minister of Education Kiyose which was widely reported in Japanese newspapers on May 2, 1956. Minister Kiyose is reported to have said that even though the mass bowing toward the Emperor's Palace by schools is contrary to the present Constitution, "We needn't be too scrupulous about it as long as we act within our common sense."

We fear that Minister Kiyose fails to see deeply into the problem of religious freedom. To him the problem seems to be merely one of wisely escaping from the foreign provisions in the "MacArthur Constitution" which, it would seem, he believes to have been imposed on Japan by the victorious allied powers. Contrary to such superficial thinking, the real issue is far wider than Japan and much older than the various postwar directives issued by the Supreme Commander for Allied Powers regulating the separation of Shintoism from the State. The deep and universal issue is whether or not the government leaders of Japan today intend to continue to protect the God-given right of individuals to full and undiminished freedom of thought and conscience, or whether they by one device or another seek to overthrow those rights now written in the Constitution.

Take for example the Minister of Education's admission that on the Emperor's birthday some schools in Japan did force all students to do *Kyujo Yohai*. Now, let us inquire, suppose there were Christian students in the school, or suppose Christian teachers were on the staff of such schools. What if these Christians had been loyal to their faith by refusing to bow to the Palace? What would have happened? Is there any thought on the part of Minister Kiyose and his fellow leaders to see that minority groups are protected from mass control in matters of conscience? Is it his intention to cancel Article 20 of the Constitution? "Freedom of religion is guaranteed to all. No religious organization shall receive any privileges from the State, nor exercise any political authority. No person shall be compelled to take part in any religious act, celebration, rites or practice. The State and its organs shall refrain from religious education or any other religious activity."

The dangerous spirit of indifference, even contempt, for these Constitutional liberties will not be reassuring to friendly nations abroad. If the revision of the Constitution means that all these liberties are to be wiped out, then truly Christians everywhere in the world cannot but be distressed. We do not believe it is the desire of Japanese people to bring back into government and politics the Shinto monopoly which characterized the course of the Japanese Empire prior to 1945. We plead with the people of Japan to defend their precious liberties gained at so great a price of suffering during the last war.

The best memorial for the heroic dead of this nation and the finest basis for the moral training of her children in the schools of Japan, cannot be found in a return to the mistaken totalitarianism of the past. Rather, the true hope of Japan is toward a richer freedom for all under the wise provisions of the present Constitution.

Christians ask no special favors. We do not ask a thing for ourselves which we do not also desire for others. Our only prayer is that expressed in Luke's Gospel, chapter 1:74-75: "That He would grant unto us, that we being delivered out of the hand of our enemies might serve Him without fear, in holiness and righteousness before Him, all the days of our life."

Two months later a more surprising protest against the reactionary trend in the educational field was directed to the Ministry of Education. This was a statement prepared and signed by 250 scholars, consisting chiefly of members of the Historical Academy of Japan. Forthrightly it declared that there ought not to be any "revival of reverse course education in history." The startling aspect of it was that one of the signatories was the emperor's brother, His Imperial Highness Prince Mikasa, a scholar of early Oriental history and a member of the academy. Two days later, the *Mainichi Shimbun* carried the account of a news interview with the prince about this matter, the following being some translated excerpts:

"As the Education Ministry itself is positively thinking of the 'reverse course' we have warned them that there is a danger of their throwing away the ripe fruits which were born of much travail, in their thus taking the present occasion as an opportunity to revise the educational system.... There is already an idea to interpret

the record of the *Kojiki* [A.D. 712, record of ancient Shinto mythology] as history, which will bring a blind belief in it. A pamphlet with this intent has already been sent me. Therefore my signature to the statement against this tendency was a means of taking precautionary measures against this." When asked, "What basic attitude and what method do you recommend for teaching Japanese history in the schools?" the prince replied: "Of course, a patriotic spirit is a desirable thing. It is not always bad to foster a patriotic spirit by learning the history of our country. However, it is wrong to try to instill a patriotic spirit by changing a tradition into a fixed fact, as we did in Japan before the war. For

The crown prince marries a commoner on April 10, 1959

example, teaching that 'Japan has 2,600 years of history since her foundation,' et cetera. We should face these things as they are. In this respect, Japanese history education after the war has at least started along the right lines, and with another effort we may make sure of the ancient history of Japan in a scientific way."[16]

The prince's reputation as a courageous and outspoken critic of a distortion of history was to become even more firmly established three years later, with the publication of his book *Emperors, Graves and the Common People—The Dawn of the Orient*, already referred to, in which he declared the conduct of the war in China had clearly revealed that it certainly was not a "holy war." That Japan should have as a spokesman for freedom one who is the brother of the emperor who, at the same time, has the courage to resist openly the prevailing current of his country, is one of the most hopeful portents for the continuance of the nation's freedom.

Censorship of the Press

Throughout the first decade after the war the English-language press showed an outstanding fairness and freedom from censoring tendencies in their handling of letters to the editors, a circumstance still largely true. This was particularly true of the *Nippon Times* (new name, *Japan Times*) which carried many letters of a controversial nature in the church–state controversy. Early in 1957, however, an incident occurred that reflected a change of policy probably due to a change in editorship. The head of the Japan Bible Society, a former general secretary of the NCC, had witten a lengthy letter to the editor in which he had given the typical NCC presentation of the origin of the Kyodan. The present author wrote a letter in reply, stating the actual circumstances behind the Kyodan's origin but the letter failed to appear. Eventually he phoned the newspaper about it and was told by the head of the department, a Kyodan member and strong supporter of the NCC, that it was the *Times*'s policy to promote good relations between the Japanese and foreign constituency and that discussion of the Kyodan's origin from the different points of view of a missionary and a Japanese churchman was not likely to do this. Thus it had been decided not to carry the letter.

It was pointed out to the *Japan Times* representative that the letter was written objectively and depended largely on Japanese sources for its material so as not to represent just a foreign point of view. Further, he was reminded that to refuse to carry an answer to a letter on the grounds given was hardly in keeping with the *Times*'s banner slogan, "All the News Without Fear or Favor." Finally, it was said that the best way for the press to preserve its own freedom was to exercise that freedom and not to practice censorship by refusing to publish both sides of a story in an effort to please some of its readers. All this was to no avail, however, although shortly afterwards two brief paragraphs of the letter were published. Since the letter deals with matters which are of historical import, it is reproduced here and the reader can judge for himself whether or not the *Times* was justified in not carrying it.

Dear Sir: — Mr. Miyakoda, of the Japan Bible Society, formerly an NCC General Secretary, in a lengthy letter to the *Japan Times* of January 14th, stated, "The United Church came about in God's providence without any pressure from the Government." This is a rather startling "interpretation" of history in the light of the facts of seventeen years ago. Those who lived through those years of government intimidation and ecclesiastical fear will know just how out of focus it is. Some other Japanese writers have been more frank about the situation of that time. One such is Professor Hiyane who wrote on this subject in the *Japan Christian Quarterly* Summer issue of 1952. His article opened with this assertion:

"It is frequently said at home as well as abroad that the Church of Christ in Japan was compelled to be established under a totalitarian policy of the government during an abnormal period. We shall not attempt to apologize for the fact that its foundation was partly due to the policy of the war-time government with respect to religions, but our purpose here is to describe the historical background of the movement for church union."

Government pressure was very obviously an important factor. In fact, in spite of there being from the beginning Christians who desired a united church, the gulf between modernists, with their liberal theology, and evangelicals, with their Biblical one, as well as the differences arising over church government, apostolic succession and the subject of baptism, made a church union of anything like the wartime proportions impossible, except for government pressure. To this Prof. Hiyane also alludes when he goes on to discuss the Religious Bodies Law passed through the two houses of the Diet by the Hiranuma Cabinet of 1939.

He points out that under this law twenty-three different Christian Church groups could register and obtain government recognition, but that the Religious Department of the Education Ministry privately ruled that Churches must have 5,000 members and fifty churches to be approved. This ruling meant that only seven denominations could obtain the approval and immediately put pressure on the others either to unite with them, or together, so as to receive the desired recognition. Even this, however, was not enough to overcome the antipathy to church union, as Mr. Hiyane points out. "But the Protestant Church, with its may denominations, was not able to open the way (to union) under the existing conditions at that time, even to face the practice of the Religious Bodies Law," he wrote. His very next paragraph, however, introduces the new factor which suddenly brought the union to pass.

"On July 21, 1940, with the appearance of the third Konoe Cabinet, political parties were dissolved and the totalitarian system became a reality. What was oppressed was liberalism, and on the assumption that Christianity was liberal and individualistic, the churches as well as Christian people were suspected by the government. As Japan became isolated from the whole world, Christian churches were criticized as the hothouse of spies because churches had relations with America and England. On August 6, the staff members of the Salvation Army were arrested on suspicion that they could not avoid acting as spies because of their relation to their headquarters in England. The Episcopal Church, considering what had happened to the Salvation Army and sensing the danger of oppression, decided to undertake self-support immediately. Thus as self-support was considered an urgent practice in each denomination, those which were supported by a foreign mission board very earnestly sought to solve this problem. Consequently, some interested persons of both the Congregational and Methodist Churches held a consultation meeting on August 17 regarding church union."

Does this indeed look as if there were no government pressure on the churches? Pastors were shocked and frightened by what happened to the Salvation Army. When military officials, the much feared gendarmes, came to them without written orders but, standing with their hands on their swords, told them that if they were to free themselves of the suspicion of espionage they must sever their connections with foreign finances or missionaries and unite into one Japanese Church, "self-support" and "church union" became "urgent" considerations! This method of intimidating the Church is typical of totalitarian governments whether it was the Shinto-militarist presurrender one here, or the present Communist one in China where the national "Self-Support, Aid-Korea, Fight-America Church of Christ in China" was pressed into union. The totalitarian government of 1940 wanted a totalitarian church, united as one, so it could issue its directives to the Church (such as that requiring a palace-worshipping rite, *kyujo yohai*, at every service) through one superintendent, and hold him responsible to issue them in the name of the Church rather than the government.

At the end of the war, before any missionaries had returned, many pastors and churches began to escape the Kyodan. The *Kaikaku Ha* (Reformed Church) was formed early in 1946 by pastors and churches which withdrew as early as October 1945. The reason was their conviction concerning the Kyodan's theological latitudinarianism and shameful accommodation to Shinto ideology, and certainly not just financial gain. In 1950, a large group of former Presbyterians withdrew and formed the *Shin Nikki*, giving as one of their chief reasons the fact that the Kyodan was getting about half of its income from America! This Church is not financed from abroad. This is the very opposite from Mr. Miyakoda's inference that churches left the Kyodan to please missionaries and to obtain their financial help. Some may have left for such reasons but others had far nobler goals. In any case, a Kyodan leader is hardly in a position to be critical in this regard!

The Kyodan had its day to present the nation and the world with a "united front," but did it show that in this "the only way to success lay," as Mr. Miyakoda indicates? Never in history has a successful church, judged from spiritual standards, held that the way to convert the "heathen" was to join them by participating in their religious rites. In 1936 the NCC declared "the Shinto Shrine is nonreligious" in approval of Christians doing obeisance before the Shinto shrines. Mr. Miyakoda speaks of "the great gathering at Aoyama Gakuin on Oct. 22, 1940" (the program indicates it met on the 17th), with obvious approval. Yet the program included the singing of a specially written hymn of praise to the Emperor in which this Christian assembly adopted the Shinto ideology and sang of him as being "in direct succession to the Sun Goddess." Afterwards many of the leaders went out and bowed before the Meiji Shrine. There was strong "pressure from the government," direct and indirect, in bringing these events to pass and the Kyodan into existence. The NCC is now writing a history of the Christian movement in Japan for the coming centennial year. Will it indeed be a "history" if it does not give these facts a more unbiased interpretation than has this letter to the *Japan Times*?[17]

Shushin, Japanese Ethics, Returns to the Schools

The battle to prevent the revision of the Fundamental Education Law was lost in the Diet in 1956. One of the first changes introduced following that event was announced as being the reintroduction of *shushin* (ethics) into the school curriculum. The next fall the following story appeared in the press.

The Shizuoka Prefectual Board of Education instructed all Junior High Schools under its jurisdiction to institute weekly one hour ethics lessons from next month. It will be the first time ethics will be taught in Japanese classrooms in that prefecture since the old ethics courses were abolished in the democratization of the nation's education after the war. The Board's decision to institute the controversial ethics lessons jumped the gun on any formal decision by the Ministry of Education. The Ministry's Curriculum Council recently recommended that ethics courses should be revived in all primary and junior high schools from next April. The Shizuoka Prefectural Teacher's Union is strongly critical of the Board's decision. It says the ethics course is designed only to instill a sense of duty and obedience and makes no mention of basic human rights and peace.[18]

This story points out one of the deep problems underlying Japanese postwar society. In the prewar educational curriculum, the point of ethical orientation, or the *summum bonum* (supreme good), could be summarized as being "live and work for the glory of the emperor." The emperor's postwar renunciation of deity,

Education Minister Matsunaga visits a shushin (ethics) class just after 1958 reintroduction to schools.

however, coupled with the democratization of the nation, has largely eliminated this as an ethical *summum bonum*. Now a conflict exists. The conservatives, so the socialists charge, wish to base ethical instruction on the feudalistic idea, closely akin to the prewar concept, of filial piety—that is, of making the highest good to be dutiful obedience to the family system (with its feudalistic concepts), which would in turn lead back to the emperor as the father of the nation. The socialists, who predominate in the teachers' unions, on the other hand, wish to make the *summum bonum* the service of humanity and the cause of peace (with strong Communist implications and interpretations). This situation faces the Christian with the stirring challenge of confronting men with the need of surrendering their lives to Christ and recognizing man's *summum bonum* to be "to glorify God and enjoy Him for ever."

It was not long before Christians began to realize what use some old-time educators were going to make of the *shushin* instruction, and to raise their voices in protest. In November a story in a Kobe newspaper reported a school excursion of Kobe children to Ise Shrine with the following description: "The most important part of the schedule was the visits to the Inner and Outer Shrines. Before the excursions, some of the schools gave preparatory instruction to the children on how to bow. In spite of all this, the impression received by the children from the visits was unexpectedly small. Concerning the worship, there were some who led the children to stand in a row and asked them to worship with the 2 bows, 2 hand claps and 1 bow ... just like we did in olden times."[19] Part of the preparatory instruction, it was indicated, included a mimeographed handbook in which such instruction as the following appeared: "At the time of worship, clothing must be neatly fixed. When worshipping the shrine (*Jinja o ogamu toki wa*), perform two bows, two hand claps, and one bow."[20]

A Pastor Protests the Constitutional Infringement

Following this news story publication, Pastor Kiiche Matsuda, of a Reformed Church in Kobe, took the lead in preparing a formal protest for the Hyogo Ken Ministerial Council to submit to the Kobe Board of Education. He sent a copy of this to the *Bible Times*, together with a news story, from which the following quotation is taken:

The sixth grade children of a Kobe municipal school left for an excursion to Ise district last November 4th (1957). Before starting for Ise this school gave instructions on shrine worship; in Ise all the children were commanded to worship. Three of my Sunday school children (two of these three were children of church members) participated in this trip but they refused to worship. I learned of this afterwards and thanked the Lord that He gave them courage and confidence. But I was shocked by the importance of the issue. As I expected, I later learned that many Kobe schools were involved in this matter. We learned of the extent of the problem from the report of the Kobe *Shimbun* of Nov. 27, and also from the distribution of handbooks to the children (which contained these worship instructions). We never dreamed that such a situation could happen again after the war. And this was done openly by a public school of one of the five biggest cities in Japan, in Kobe, an international port. And the worship was not done with an ordinary bow, but done with 2 bows, 2 hand-claps, and one bow. This was clearly a religious act. This was done by the children in unison. We are greatly shocked.

Before the war the shrines were not regarded as religious, and their control was shifted from the Ministry of Education to the Ministry of Home Affairs. However, since the war the shrines fall under the religious corporation law. This means that Ise shrine is a "religious" place and it must not be given special treatment by the state. (Except for the special relationship it has with the Imperial house.) Therefore, regardless of the feelings of the average man, it is a sheer violation of article 20 of the constitution, and of article 9 of the Education law, when a public school drills children on how to worship, prior to an excursion, and then leads them to worship in unison before the shrine. A public school which is supposed to teach obedience to the law violated it.

Since many schools in Kobe were involved in this, it is easy to imagine that a similar situation may prevail all over Japan. The "Moral Education" of the Ministry of Education deserves the close scrutiny of many. My doubts about the real purpose of this "Moral Education" were deepened by a recent experience.

As the head of a kindergarten, I received an invitation to a research report meeting under the sponsorship of Kobe University Education Department. The program included a lecture entitled "The problematic point in the education curriculum," by Mr. Iwao Utsumi, the Inspector from the Ministry of Education. I considered this meeting a good opportunity to know the opinion of the Ministry of Education relating to the problem so, in spite of some obstacles, I attended the meeting.

As I expected, the lecture dealt with the problem of "Moral Education." Following the lecture was a question period of about twenty minutes. I was granted permission and asked the following question: "What do you think about the fact that a public school in Hyogo ken drilled the children on how to worship before going to Ise, and then had 'moral education' include such practices?" Here are the answers he gave:

"1) I first have to check the opinion of the superintendent.

"2) This is a matter which is under consideration by the deliberative committee of the Ministry of Education, so I cannot answer."

Mr. Utsumi then asked me why I was asking such a question. I replied that what had been done was clearly a violation of the Constitution and the Education law. Mr. Utsumi then strongly affirmed that Ise Shrine does not fall into a religious category, "but is a beautiful custom from ancient times." I urged him that if the matter is not settled, there must not be permitted such violation. I asked that he express my objection to the deliberation committee. Mr. Utsumi promised that he would do so; I hope he has fulfilled that promise. I reminded him how special treatment (for shrines) had poisoned our country and suppressed both the freedom of religion and the freedom of speech; I emphasized the evil of such policy.

It would have been logical for him to have assured me that the matter was important and that he would prefer not to give an answer until after investigation; it would seem that he might well have expressed a suspicion that the Consitution had been violated. But instead, Inspector Utsumi took the attitude that the matter was no problem at all (with respect to the violation of the constitution). Worse, he defined the shrine as "not a religion, but a beautiful custom from ancient times." He implied that the worship by the children was right, and his speech indicated an attitude of no special concern about the problem. I did not go to the meeting to find out his personal opinion; out of a feeling of true patriotism I sought a public answer. I think the view expressed is the view of the Ministry itself. If the view of the Ministry is different from the view expressed, Inspector Utsumi must take the responsibility.

Once this was a problem which concerned our Christian faith only and it was a battle to be fought by us. But now the Constitution is changed, granting freedom. The Constitution is not the constitution of Christians only; it is the Constitution of all the people. The Constitution and the law chosen by us say "No" to this [violation]. To protest the violation of the laws and to protect them, is this not the duty of the people in a democratic country? We must speak with a strong voice that it is a violation of the Constitution and the Education law when any public school teaches or practises shrine worship.[21]

We shall bring this chapter to a close with a quotation from an editorial written about this patriotic action of Pastor Matsuda.

More than six years have passed since Mr. Young wrote an editorial for the *Bible Times*, "The Road Back," in which he said: "It is very clear that there is pressure from every side to lead the nation back to the place where it is required to show one's patriotism by participating in certain acts of the nationally observed religion of Shinto." The Kobe case, which is dealt with in this issue in some detail, deserves the careful consideration of every Christian in Japan; it shows that it is even more apparent today that Japan is on the road back.

The resurgence of Shinto comes with a cry for moral education. But Shinto is almost divorced from morality. In the town of Toba (in Mie Prefecture) a brothel keeper has just turned Shinto priest. In accordance with the anti-prostitution law which takes full effect in April (1958) Kiku Miyase closed out his business.

As it happened, the shrine was without a chief priest and Mr. Miyase received a unanimous call. It is commendable that those in such a business are turning to other pursuits, but the ease with which the transition was made shows that Pastor Matsuda has more than one reason to protest the identification of Shinto with moral education.

Mr. Matsuda makes a good point when he says that "out of a feeling of true patriotism" he sought an answer from the inspector of education. Many Christians realize that there is no greater patriotic service they can render their country than to preserve within it freedom of religion and freedom of speech. Every Christian ought to rejoice that there are men who understand the real meaning of religious freedom. The pressure again to define the shrines as nonreligious is a serious threat against religious freedom. Early in February the writer had an opportunity to ask a priest at Yasukuni Shrine his view as to whether Shinto was a religion or only a beautiful custom, as was claimed in the Kobe case. The priest replied that if you define religion in a certain way, as for example a system of theology with canons, etc. Shinto might not fall under the category of a religion. "But," the priest concluded, "probably Shinto should be called a religion." Christians must pray that the Ministry of Education may reject any official future falsification aimed to put Shinto in a nonreligious category for favored treatment.

God opened the door in a new way for getting the Gospel to this great nation after World War II. He can hold open the door of opportunity and in this the Christian can rejoice. But God used human instruments. Fear at this time can keep Christians from following the patriotic example of Mr. Matsuda and such men as the pastor opposing *Kigensetsu*. Let every Christian pray for courage to do his part to press upon his neighbors and his nation that true patriotism involves a protest of violations of personal freedoms guaranteed in the constitution.[22]

---

1. *Time,* the weekly news magazine, January 17, 1955.

2. *Nippon Times*, January 4, 1955, Tokyo.

3. *Nippon Times,* Mainichi, *Asahi Evening News*, and *Yomiuri Japan News*.

4. *Nippon Times,* January 12, 1955.

5. *Asahi Evening News*, January 14, 1955, Tokyo.

6. *Eternity, Magazine of Christian Truth*, March 1955, Philadelphia.

7. JBCC News Release of April 1955.

8. *Japan Christian Yearbook,* 1956, p. 29, Tokyo, Japan.

9. FECCC Karuizawa Minutes, *op. cit.,* p. 31.

10. *Nippon Times,* March 27, 1956, Tokyo.

11. *Asahi Weekly,* April 29, 1956, Tokyo.

12. *Ibid.,* April 23, 1956.

13. *Nippon Times,* April 8, 1956, Tokyo.

14. *Jinja Shimpo,* December 5, 1955, quoted from *The Bible Times,* Vol. VI, No. 1, p. 9, translated by Hideo Nagase and the author.

15. *Nippon Times,* May 2, 1956, Tokyo.

16. JBCC News Release, No. 20, translated from the *Mainichi Shimbun,* October 2, 1953, by Mr. Masanaga and Samuel E. Boyle, the editor.

17. *The Bible Times,* Vol. VII, No. 1, 1957, pp. 21-2.

18. *Asahi Evening News,* November 13, 1957, Tokyo.

19. *Kobe Shimbun,* November 27, 1957, as quoted in *The Bible Times,* Vol. VIII, No. 1, 1958, p. 4, translated by Makito Goto and Philip R. Foxwell.

20. Mimeographed Excursion Handbook, *The Bible Times, ibid.,* p. 8.

21. Kiichi Matsuda, "Red Light on the Educational Road," *The Bible Times,* Vol. VIII, No. 1, 1958, pp. 2-3, translated by Makito Goto and Philip R. Foxwell.

22. Philip R. Foxwell, "The Road Back," guest editorialist in *The Bible Times,* Vol. VIII, No. 1, 1958, p. 1.

15

What of the Future?

Ｈistory has a way of repeating itself, it is said. Will it do so again in Japan? As we have traced the course of the conflict between the two empires of Christian church and pagan state, we have observed that twice the nation has responded to the Christian message brought to its shores by rejection—arbitrary rejection of its right to free existence in Japan. Nor did the island empire escape severe penalties for these rejections. In the 17th century, with the utmost exacting and ruthless measures, the nation was isolated from Christ and His gospel and thereby isolated from the enlightenment and progress the gospel, and the civilizations recognizing it, had brought to the world. In the 20th century, Japan tried to isolate its youth from instruction in the Way of Christ, turning them out into a modern world with a primitive ideology, key points of which were pride and vengeance, and watched in dismay as they took the nation to disaster. Must this tragic cycle be repeated a third time? What of the future?

"As we seek to establish the cause of Christ in Japan, knowing that we have the Word of God to guide us and the King of kings to rule us, 'let us not be weary in well doing; for in due season we shall reap, if we faint not.'"

The future? The future is in the hands of God, the Christian will say. True, but that must not be said in the interests of escaping the responsibility of trying to influence that future for good. God works through human instrumentality. It is the Christian's responsibility to seek to be that instrument. The cause of Christ in Japan is in great need of such instruments. They are the ones with whom, in the providence of God, the future rests.

If there is to develop in Japan a church of the future, free from compromise with the national polytheism without and modern theology within, then there must be an increase of the kind of instruments for God which Professor Yanagita calls the "Wrestling type" of Christian.[1] In his essay he mentions four types of professing Christians in Japan. There is the "Apostate type," illustrated by the Mukyokai leader Nobuo Odagiri, who wrote "Is Christ God?" in which he denied our Lord's deity. It has been estimated that 80 percent to 90 percent of those baptized in Japan later leave the Christian faith. Then there is the "Compromising type." A Shinto priest has written that he believes any true Japanese must be such. "Some of the shrine's *ujiko* (parishioners) have, since the war, become Christians. Are they reluctant to contribute to the shrine? The answer given is a firm and confident, no. These newly converted Christians all made it clear that there was no reason for them to cut off their relationship with the shrine even if they became Christians. In other words, 'they are always Japanese at heart even if they follow a foreign religion,' declared a priest. It is physically impossible for them to become complete Christians."[2] The priest's testimony is too true for a vast number but he was reckoning without the regenerating power of the Holy Spirit who has transformed many in Japan as He has elsewhere.

The third type mentioned by the professor is the "Escape type," typified by the neo-orthodox and some evangelicals, he says. Finally, there is the "Wrestling type." Here are the true Protestants, men who believe in testifying for (*pro*) the truth and protesting against the error which would undermine it. They have heard the call to evangelize Japan with the gospel of salvation, and with zeal seek to do it, but they know this is not all. It is the whole counsel of God which must be proclaimed for the glory of God and the vindication of His righteousness. They know the problems of ministering the holy gospel in a pagan land cannot be escaped but must be wrestled with, in the power of the Holy Spirit, and overcome without compromise. They know that a Christian cannot have two supreme allegiances, and devotion to God as their sovereign Lord is supreme with them. Love of Him is their highest motive. The wrestling type recognize as part of their responsibility to the God they love their need of trying to protect the church from compromise. They know, too, that a church that will not practice discipline will not long maintain its purity.

First edition of Hepburn's Japanese-English dictionary, 1867

A wrestler knows the value of thorough preparation. Those of this type, whether missionary or pastor, usually have a high regard for educational as well as spiritual preparation. For their encounter with the trained forces of unbelief, as well as for reaching all levels with their various problems, both of these attainments are necessary. The more of such men there are, the brighter the future will look. If the gospel is to be firmly implanted in Japan, it is imperative that many young Japanese men be thoroughly trained for the ministry, in evangelistic zeal, Bible-centered teaching, doctrinal awareness, and willingness to wrestle for the Lord against the forces opposing His Church, both within and without.[3] It was the few, but highly trained,

Reformed missionary Rev. G.F. Verbeck (1859) and his first class of samurai sons in Nagasaki

consecrated men—the Hepburns, Browns, Verbecks—who made such a profound impact on this nation at the beginning of the Protestant centennial. In contrast, one can think of a postwar mission board that took the extreme position of sending almost anyone who wanted to come as a Christian missionary, and within a few years had sent some sixty missionaries. Almost nothing of lasting worth was accomplished by this group, in spite of the great sums of money which must have been spent, and now only one or two of them still remain in Japan.

As the struggle to turn the nation back to the old paths intensifies in the days ahead, the courageous witness of men like Pastor Matsuda of Kobe will be of the greatest significance. The reactionary Shinto nationalists will go just as far as they think the public will let them go in turning the clock back and infringing the constitution. If no such voice of protest is raised, as was lifted by this pastor and his associates, and taken to the public and the proper ministerial authority, then religious freedom will be lost to the Christian by default. Letters to the Christian periodicals of the modernists and indifferentists, such as Pastor Atari's protesting the compromising statements of Archbishop Yashiro of the Episcopal Church, also are of great value. When a prominent churchman advocates the restoration of a pagan holiday (*Kigensetsu*), the church needs to be warned. "*Kigensetsu* emerged from the ideology of the centrality of the Imperial House. We must reckon that the revival of it is directly connected with such ideology and the deification of the Emperor."[4]

Letters in the English-language press, such as that of "Vigilant" protesting the police department's joint sponsorship with Shinto priests of ceremonies dedicating newly installed traffic lights, are certainly worthwhile. Missionaries who take the position that as guests in the land they cannot make such public comments forget they are here to teach by word and example, and this example of speaking out is much needed. The letter stated, "This morning policemen came and erected an open pavilion, of red and white bunting, on the sidewalk in order to hold a ceremony to dedicate the new stop light. A Shinto altar was erected in the pavilion, and food and *sake* [wine] placed upon it…. When such is sponsored by the police, on public property and with the money of taxpayers, is this not a direct violation of the Constitution? Such violations cannot be excused by calling them 'custom' or 'nonreligious.' Shintoism under the law is religious and has no special rights or privileges."

Those who break the law, and the constitution, do not like to have their actions brought to light and held up to public rebuke. Especially do they not like to have it called to the attention of the world in the English-language press. It is well known that protests published there get results and have a salutary influence. Such writings of the men of the wrestling type have a real contribution to make in the protection of the future.

If the new church in Japan is to develop in freedom, the Christian must recognize not only his responsibility to wrestle for the preservation of the church's purity but also, in so far as he can, to wrestle for the preservation of the nation's freedom. The great principles of freedom guaranteed in the postwar constitution are in jeopardy. The threat comes not only from the reactionaries, both left and right, but from those who espouse to be the friends of democracy. In the majestic providence of God, democracy (and therefore religious freedom) is preserved in Japan today by a precarious balance of political powers, those of the rightists, the Shinto nationalists who would drag the nation back to the days of the police state, and the leftists who resist them. Among the latter there is a strong element of Communists who, if they could have their way, would shackle the nation with a police state probably even more ruthless in its suppression of a free church. It is this writer's opinion, however, that the traditional sentiment of the Japanese people will keep them from turning voluntarily to this ideology, unless it is thrust upon them by military conquest as it was upon the Chinese.

The source of the greatest threat to democracy and freedom in Japan today seems to go back to a very basic situation. There does not appear to be a genuine belief that democratic processes will really work. This is apparently the case in both the conservative Liberal-Democratic Party, which seeks "to protect democracy" in Japan by changing the constitution and increasing the powers of the government, and in the Socialist Party, which seeks to preserve democracy under the slogan "Protect the Constitution." If the conservative party really believes in democratic procedures, why does it increase bureaucratic powers by revising the Education Law, and seek the revision of the Religious Juridical Persons Law, the Broadcasting Law and now the Police Duties Execution Law? These democratic laws, under a democratic constitution, are quite sufficient to protect the people's democratic

Diet riot as socialists try force to prevent Education Law revision, June 1, 1956

rights if properly adminstered. A democratic society cannot flourish under strong, stultifying control regulations.

A struggling democracy sees the socialists forcibly block the House Speaker in the anti-Police Law revision conflict, October 1958

On the other hand, if the Socialists really believe in the efficacy of democratic processes, why do they resort to physical force and strongarm measures in the Diet rather than relying on parliamentary procedures in their conflict with the reactionaries? In the battle to preserve democracy in Germany in the early 1930s, fought between those who sought to preserve democracy and the Reds, it was the Nazi facists who gained and came to power. Herein lies the danger to Japan's democracy today. Democracy cannot be preserved by undemocratic methods. Strongarm measures will inevitably turn the people against those who seek to preserve democracy by them. When the Communists tried force in the May Day riot of 1952, they lost popular support, which they have never regained. The Socialists too, if they persist in "direct action" measures, will lose that support for their battle and in the reaction the old "conservatives" will be enabled to go far in turning the clock back.

A Japanese political analyst has pointed out that during the past years the left-wing in the Socialist Party has greatly increased. Eight years ago the right-wingers numbered 32 against 16 left-wingers in the Diet. Today it is 104 left-wingers to 67 right-wingers. He also points out that affiliated members of the Sohyo [large labor union, Red led] "occupy as many as 86 seats, or almost one-third of the total strength of the 243 Socialist seats in the Diet"[5] He makes two significant observations. "Such being the current circumstances, it is but natural that the Socialist Party should continue in its leftist course, much against the wish of the public and its more sensible leaders."[6] Also, "Unless the Socialist Party readjusts its too obviously anti-American, pro-Communist policy, it cannot possibly expect to secure increased votes."[7] He also quotes from a resolution of Zenro [the second largest labor organization], which states, "The worst of its [the Socialist Party's] shortcomings is its lack of independence, which invites the general suspicion that it is under the influence of some undesirable pressure groups

[Sohyo is implied] and foreign countries" [China and the USSR are implied].[8]

As the Christian, concerned with the task of bringing the precious gospel to Japan, considers this picture of the political and religious situation here, he can be either discouraged or encouraged depending on the depth of his faith in the greatness of God. We who are here in Japan are here to labor for Him regardless of the circumstances, for our God is Lord over all circumstances. Let us then labor manfully onward like Nehemiah, building the wall upward even while ever prepared to protect it from the Lord's enemies. Let us learn the lessons from history, the stage on which God's ultimate plan is gradually being unfolded, and realize anew that eternal vigilance is the price of freedom. Further, that in the conflict between the two empires of Christ and polytheism we must not fail to discern what can properly be rendered to the non-

Building Tokyo Tower

Christian state and what to God alone. As we seek to establish the cause of Christ in Japan, knowing that we have the WORD OF GOD to guide us and the KING OF KINGS to rule us, "let us not be weary in well doing; for in due season we shall reap, if we faint not."

An expanding city, the old and the new, church and Shinto shrine, symbols of the Two Empires. To which does the future belong?

1. Tomonobu Yanagita, "Problems of the Evangelical Mission to Japan, Today and Tomorrow," in *The Bible Times*, Vol. VIII, No. 3, p. 6, 1958.

2. *Japan News*, September 16, 1950.

3. The Japan Christian Theogical Seminary of Tokyo was founded for this purpose and is dedicated to this goal, as is also the Japan Christian Presbyterian Church.

4. F. Atari, in the *Kirisuto Shimbun*, No. 521, translated by P. Foxwell and M. Goto, *The Bible Times,* Vol. VIII, No. 1, 1958, p. 12.

5. Tatsuo Mitarai, "Post-Election Development in Politics," *Contemporary Japan*, Vol. XXV, No. 8, September 1958, p. 345.

6. *Ibid.*

7. *Ibid.*, p. 343.

8. *Ibid.*, p. 344.

Bibliography

Historical, of Japan

Akagi, R. Hidemichi — *Japan's Foreign Relations, 1542-1936, A Short History,* The Hokuseido Press, Tokyo, 1936.

Aston, W.G. — *Hideyoshi's Invasion of Korea*, 1881.

Brinkley, F. & Kikuchi, Dairoku — *A History of the Japanese People,* The Encyclopedia Britannica Co., New York, 1914.

Bryan, J. Ingram, *The Civilization of Japan*, William & Norgate, 1927.

Callahan, J.M. — *American Relations in the Pacific and the Far East from 1784 to 1900*, 1901.

Clement, E.W. — *A Short History of Japan*, The University of Chicago Press, Chicago, 1915.

Ienaga, Saburo — *History of Japan*, Tourist Library Vol. 15, Japan Travel Bureau, Tokyo, 1953.

James, D.H. — *Rise and Fall of the Japanese Empire*, Allen & Unwin, 1951.

McLaren, W.W. — *Political History of Japan During the Meiji Era*, 1916.

Murdock, James — *A History of Japan*, III vols., Kegan, Trench, Trubner & Co., London, 1926.

Reischauer, Edwin O. — *Japan, Past and Present*, Charles E. Tuttle Co., Tokyo, 1946.

Sansom, G.B. Japan, *A Short Cultural History,* 1931; Revised Edition 1943, Appleton, Century, Crofts, Inc., N.Y.

Sansom, G.B. — *The Western World and Japan*, Cresset, 1950.

Sansom, G.B. — *Japan in World History*, Institute of Pacific Relations, New York, 1951.

Tamura, Dr. Kosaka — "Japan's Foreign Relations," *Contemporary Japan*, from Vol. XXIII, Nos. 1–3, 1954-'59.

Tolischus, Otto D. — *Tokyo Record*, Reynal & Hitchcock, New York, 1943.

Williams, F.W. — *A Journal of the Perry Expedition to Japan 1853-1854*, by S. Wells Williams, First Interpreter of the Expedition, 1910.

Historical, of Christianity in Japan

Boxer, C.R. — *The Christian Centuries in Japan 1549-1650*, University of California Press, 1951.

Cary, Otis — *A History of Christianity in Japan*, Protestant Mission Press, New York, Fleming H. Revell Co., 1909.

Minutes of the First General Assembly of the FECCC, 1951.

Minutes of the Second General Assembly of the FECCC, Karuizawa; Singapore, 1953.

Omura, Haruo — "History of the Presbyterian Church in Japan," in *The Bible Times*, Vol. VII, 1957.

Pieters, Albertus — *Mission Problems in Japan*, The Board of Publication, New York, 1912.

Proceedings of the General Conference of the Protestant Missionaries of Japan held in Osaka, April 1883; Yokohama.

Proceedings of the General Conference of Protestant Missions in Japan, Tokyo, 1900.

Ritter, H. — *A History of the Protestant Missions in Japan*. Revised by D.E. Greene. Methodist Publishing House, 1898

Yanagita, T. — *A Short History of Christianity in Japan*, Seisho Tosho Kankokai, Sendai, Japan, 1957.

Biographical

Aoyoshi, Dr. K. — *Masahisa Uemura, A Christian Leader*, Kyo Bun Kwan, Tokyo, 1940.

Ebizawa, Norimachi — *Japanese Witnesses for Christ*, Lutterworth Press, London, 1957.

Griffis, W.E. — *A Maker of the New Orient*, Samuel Robbins Brown, New

York, Fleming H. Revell Co., 1902.

Griffis, W. — *Hepburn of Japan,* Westminster Press, 1913.

Griffis, W. — *Verbeck of Japan, A Citizen of No Country*, New York, Fleming H. Revell Co.

Jennings, Raymond P. — *Jesus, Japan, and Kanzo Uchimura,* Kyobun Kwan, Tokyo, 1958.

Kozaki, H: — *Reminiscences of Seventy Years*, Kyo Bun Kwan, Tokyo, 1933.

Satoh, Henry — *Lord Hotta, Pioneer Diplomat of Japan*, Tokyo, 1908.

Takaya, M. — *The Letters of Dr. J.C. Hepburn*, Toshin Shobo, Tokyo, Japan, 1955.

Uchimura, Kanzo — *The Works of Uchimura*, Vol. 15, "How I Became a Christian," Tokyo, 1895.

Interpretative

Argall, Phyllis — *My Life with the Enemy.*

Argall, Phyllis — *Prisoner in Japan*, Bles.

Axling, William — *Japan at the Midcentury: Leaves From Life*, Protestant Publishing Company, 1955.

Axling, William — *Japan on the Upward Trail*, Missionary Education Movement of the United States and Canada, New York, 1923.

Benedict, Ruth — *The Chrysanthemum and the Sword*, Charles E. Tuttle Company, Tokyo, 1946.

Baker, Richard T. — *Darkness of the Sun*, Abingdon-Cokesbury Press, New York, 1947.

Byram, Bertha S. — *Brought Before Governors for a Testimony*, Independent Board (pamphlet), Philadelphia, 1943.

Byram, Bertha S. — God's Presence in a Japanese Prison, Independent Board, (Pamphlet), Philadelphia, 1943.

Cary, Otis — *Japan and Its Regeneration,* Laymen's Missionary Movement, 1899.

Foxwell, Philip R. *Can Evangelicals Cooperate with the N.C.C.?*, JBCC Publishing Department, (pamphlet), Tokyo, 1957.

Gibney, Frank — *Five Gentlemen of Japan*, Charles E. Tuttle Co., Tokyo, 1953.

Gosden, E.W. — *Night Came to Japan*, Marshall, Morgan & Scott, London, 1951.

Government Information — *Japan for the Young*, Tourist Library Services, Tokyo, Japan, 1934.

Gulick, Sidney L. — *Evolution of the Japanese*, Fleming H. Revell Co., 1903.

Hearn, Lafcadio — *Japan, An Interpretation*, Charles E. Tuttle Co., Tokyo, 1904, Reprinted 1955.

Hearn, Lafcadio — *A Japanese Miscellany*, C.E. Tuttle Co., postwar reprint.

Holtom, D,C. — *Modern Japan and Shinto Nationalism*, University of Chicago Press, 1943; Revised 1947.

Iglehart, C.W. — *Cross and Crisis in Japan*, Friendship Press, N.Y.,1957.

Japan Christian Yearbook, Kyobun Kwan (published each year),Tokyo.

Kagawa, T. — *The Religion of Jesus*, Tokyo.

Kerr, William C. — *Japan Begins Again*, Friendship Press, New York, 1949.

Price, Willard — *Japan and the Son of Heaven*, Duell, Sloan and Pearce, New York, 1945,

Shimmura, I. — *Western Influence on Japanese History and Culture in Earlier Periods (1510-1860)*, 1936.

Toynbee, Harold — *East and West*, Oxford, 1958.

Vos, J.G. — "Christian Missions and the Civil Magistrate in the Far East," (*Westminster Theological Journal*) Vol. III, 1940; JBCC pamphlet, reprint, 1952.

Vos, J.G. — Foreign Missions Conference of N.A., A Review of its 50th Annual Report, Evangelical Fellowship, Pittsburgh, 1944.

Religious

Anesaki, Masaharu — *History of Japanese Religion,* 1930.

Aston, W.G. — *Shinto, The Way of the Gods,* 1905.

Aston, W.G. — *Nihongi: Chronicles of Japan* (translation), 1896; reprinted 1952, Allen and Unwin, Ltd., London.

Buchanan, Dr. D.C. — *Inari: Its Origin, Development, and Nature; The Transactions of the Asiatic Society of Japan*, Second Series, Vol. XII, 1935, Asiatic Society of Japan.

Bunce, William K. — *Religions in Japan,* GHQ, SCAP, C.I. and E. Sec., Religions and Cultural Resources Division report, 1948.

Callaway, T.N. — *Japanese Buddhism and Christianity*, Shinkyo Shuppansha, Protestant Publishing Co., Tokyo, 1957.

Hamada, H., ed. — *Religions in Japan at Present*, Sanwa, Tokyo, 1958.

Holtom, D.C. — *The National Faith of Japan*, The University of Chicago Press, 1937.

Kato, Genchi — *A Study of Shinto, The Religion of the Japanese Nation*, Tokyo, Japan, 1926.

Kato, Genchi — *Shinto in Essence, as Illustrated by the Faith in a Glorified Personality*, Nogi Shrine, Tokyo, 1954.

Kato, Genchi — *What Is Shinto?* (Japan Tourist Library), Tokyo, 1935.

Matsutani, Fumio — *A Comparative Study of Buddhism and Christianity*, CIIB Press, Tokyo, 1958.

Satow, Ernest — *The Revival of Pure Shinto; Ancient Japanese Rituals*, The Transactions of the Asiatic Society of Japan, reprints, Vol. II, December 1927, The Asiatic Society of Japan, Tokyo.

Wheeler, Post — *The Sacred Scriptures of the Japanese*, Henry Schuman, Inc., New York, 1952.

About the Author

John M. L. Young was born in Hamheung, Korea, of Canadian Presbyterian missionary parents, where he received his grade school education, later living in Kobe, Japan, where he graduated from the Canadian Academy. He received the degrees of B.A. (1934) and M.A. (1935) from Acadia University in Wolfville, Nova Scotia, doing his thesis work in the field of the German Reformation. He attended Westminster Theological Seminary in Philadelphia for two years and graduated in 1938 from Faith Theological Seminary, then in Wilmington, Del., to which he had transferred. That year he was ordained to the ministry of the Bible Presbyterian Church.

In the summer of 1938, he and Mrs. Young, as missionaries of the Independent Board for Presbyterian Foreign Missions, went to Harbin, Manchukuo, where (except for six months in Peking) they served until the impending war brought them home in May 1941. From early 1942 to early 1948, Mr. Young served as pastor of the Bible Presbyterian Church of Wilkes Barre, Pa., where he helped organize and was president of the Fundamental Ministerial Council of Wyoming Valley. Early in 1948 the Youngs returned to China, where they served in Nanking until the end of the year when they were transferred to Japan because of the Communist invasion.

Mr. Young helped found the Japan Christian Theological Seminary in 1949, where he has since been the professor of theology, and has served as its president since 1952. He thus writes from a background of over 25 years under the Japanese flag in four different countries.

The Two Empires in Japan
by John M. L. Young
President of the Japan Christian Theological Seminary

What reviewers have said:

"This volume deserves to be designated 'Book of the Year' in the field of foreign missions. In my judgment it is the most important book on foreign missions to appear in recent years. For sheer relevance and downright facing of realities it is outstanding. And in addition to its value as a storehouse of information and interpretation, it is interestingly written, very readable, and well illustrated with many photographs…Women's Missionary Societies could not choose a better book than this, I feel, for reading and study…. I recommend this book most heartily to all friends of foreign missions and all who love the Reformed Faith and recognize its worldwide importance."

—J.G. Vos
Dean and Editor of the Blue Banner Faith and Life

"John M.L. Young's *The Two Empires in Japan* sets out timeless principles analyzing the real conflict that resulted when the kingdom of our Lord Jesus Christ was met with the defiance of the kingdom of this world personified in the emperor of Japan and Shinto Shrine religion. He sympathetically treats the mistakes and compromises, as well as the clear-eyed sterling testimonies with their terrible price to be paid for the sake of Christ. The book sets out the history behind the modern developments and the history that he himself lived through in Japan. Young gives us not theory alone but the doctrinal groundwork for standing firm for Christ in life's hard choices under persecution and the determined push back of a resistant culture. That is why I assign this book as required reading in my course on the enterprise of missions at Reformed Presbyterian Theological Seminary in Pittsburgh…"

—Steven F. Miller
Pastor, Nassua OPC, former missionary in Eritrea,
Adjunct Professor of Missions at RPTS

"Why had the Japanese church become powerless in the face of the pressure of the government before and during World War II, and weak in spiritual battle even after the freedom of faith had been given widely? The reason was its continuous bondage to the idol worship of emperor worship, Shintoism and Buddhism. It still continues in various ways. The theory of "church growth" cannot overcome the real spiritual disease here. The spiritual battle of obedience to the Lord for each Japanese Christian in family and living is at stake, which comes from the power of His living Word. This book draws the picture well about the difficulty of being awake in Japanese society in the spiritual midnight of idol worship. Everybody who desires to pray for Japan missions needs to understand this, if you desire to pray with clear understanding and patience. We Japanese Christians appreciate your prayers very much."

—*Shigeru Takiura*
Pastor, Okamoto Keiyaku RPC, Japan Presbytery RPCNA Representative,
Kobe Theological Hall

SEMINARY TRAINING SHOULD DO
MORE THAN TEACH YOU THEOLOGY

It SHOULD TRANSFORM YOU FOR MINISTRY

REFORMED PRESBYTERIAN
THEOLOGICAL SEMINARY

(412) 731-6000 • WWW.RPTS.EDU • INFO@RPTS.EDU

PITTSBURGH, PA

Missions with a
REFORMED PERSPECTIVE

Reformed Presbyterian Missions is a short-term missions organization that provides Christians with the opportunity to serve Christ's Church throughout the world.

❀ **RP Missions seeks to approach missions** from a biblical and historic Reformed perspective.

❀ **Short-term teams work alongside established churches** and missions to ensure that follow-up and discipleship continue after the team leaves, and to encourage local congregations.

❀ **RP Missions's goal is to aid and implement the programs of the host congregations,** instead of taking our own agendas or programs to mission sites.

RP Missions provides mission opportunities for individuals, small groups, and congregations to serve God together and become better acquainted with His global Church. To find out how to become involved, please visit **www.RPMissions.org**.

Serve. Proclaim. Disciple.
www.RPMissions.org

RP Missions

Also Available from:

Crown & Covenant
P U B L I C A T I O N S

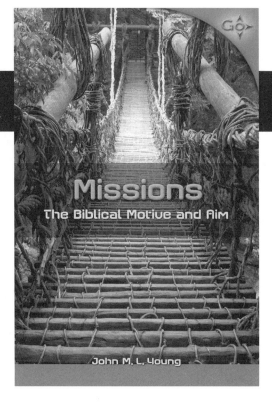

Whether you are trying to understand your calling to missions work, wanting your congregation to support missionaries more effectively, or are going on a short-term trip, this book is for you.

John M. L. Young's own mission work informed and nurtured his passion for missions, and he published his theology of missions in a series of ten pamphlets in 1964. For the first time, these studies are published in one volume.

> Missions: The Biblical Motive and Aim
> Paperback, 176 pages, Code: DS390, $10

crownandcovenant.com   (412) 241-0436